AN ASSISTANT PRINCIPAL'S GUIDE . . . INTO THE FIRE

How to Prepare for and Survive the Position

Chad Mason

Rowman & Littlefield Education
Lanham • New York • Toronto • Plymouth, UK

Published in the United States of America
by Rowman & Littlefield Education
A Division of Rowman & Littlefield Publishers, Inc.
A wholly owned subsidiary of The Rowman & Littlefield Publishing
Group, Inc.
4501 Forbes Boulevard, Suite 200, Lanham, Maryland 20706
www.rowmaneducation.com

Estover Road
Plymouth PL6 7PY
United Kingdom

British Library Cataloguing in Publication Information Available

Library of Congress Cataloging-in-Publication Data:

Mason, Chad, 1971–
  An assistant principal's guide— : into the fire how to prepare for and
survive the position / Chad Mason.
      p. cm.
  ISBN-13: 978-1-57886-671-7 (cloth : alk. paper)
  ISBN-10: 1-57886-671-5 (cloth : alk. paper)
  ISBN-13: 978-1-57886-672-4 (pbk. : alk. paper)
  ISBN-10: 1-57886-672-3 (pbk. : alk. paper)
  1. Assistant school principals. 2. School management and organization.
I. Title.
  LB2831.9.M357 2007
  372.2'012—dc22   2007020475

Printed in the United States of America

CONTENTS

1

STANDARDS IN EDUCATION

I will never forget the first advice I was given regarding the assistant principal's position by an administrative colleague, "It is the worst job in education. Do it for one or two years and move on!" Many individuals have this perception, and it is easy to see why this is the case. The assistant principal's duties, many times, are very narrow in focus. You will work primarily in three arenas—discipline of students, attendance, and garnering substitutes for teachers. As many discipline and attendance issues are negative and confrontational at times, the assistant's role can be stressful and emotionally draining. I still remember the secretary's first question during our initial meeting, "Can you yell at kids?" I thought this to be a peculiar question and was unsure as to its nature, but I answered politely and carried on the conversation.

Among dealing with those three arenas, many other items may be put on the assistant principal's plate such as the schedule for the building, supervising athletic events, or scheduling school assemblies or class meetings. In some situations, if the principal is trusting and you are fortunate, you may conduct staff evaluations, assist with creating the master schedule or scheduling of students, and gain some experience with the planning and preparation for important events such as open house or the high school graduation. The principal's role in the growth and development of the assistant cannot be overstated.

Because the principal's position has such a great impact on the assistant principal's role, it is important to have a thorough understanding of both positions. Remember, each principal/assistant principal relationship is different; but in every case, the principal is the immediate supervisor. As a result, the principal's perception of your position and how it fits into the operations of the building can hamper or assist your professional growth. It is important for you to be proactive in your studies of the administrative profession and take an active role in your own professional development.

As you begin to study the role of the administrator in the educational setting, you will begin to see how vital your own professional development will become. Further, as you progress with this reference manual and your first year in the administrative ranks, you will discover the need for professional dialogue. The principal and assistant principal, perhaps more than any positions in the district, require that you learn from those who are carrying out the same job duties as yourself. It is in this vein that you are strongly encouraged to solicit a mentor or confidant if one is not assigned to you as you begin your journey into the administrative ranks. It is not a position quickly or simply defined, especially on one's own.

In an attempt to address the complexities of the position, after two years of study, the Interstate School Leaders Licensure Consortium (ISLLC) adopted six standards for school leaders.[1] According to Fred Lindley (2003), author of *The Portable Mentor: A Resource Guide for Entry-Year Principals and Mentors*, there are two fundamental reasons for adopting the standards as the framework for your career in administration. First, the six areas genuinely encompass the enormous task of the school administrator. Second, the ISLLC standards will likely be the topic of professional development as you progress in your career. By having some familiarity with them now, you will undoubtedly have a better understanding when the opportunity arrives to review them at a later date.

As you begin to become familiar with the six ISLLC standards, it will be apparent how the assistant principal's role can change from district to district or building to building. Some of the information discussed in the standards may not be relevant to your position. As a result, it will become increasingly important for you to develop a clear understanding of the role you will have in *your* particular situation. Remember, the standards will serve as a reference framework for your maturation in the administrative arena. In addition to listing them below, I will refer to them throughout this text in discussion topics and learning scenarios so that you may become more familiar with them and understand their relation to administrative positions and your professional development.

ISLLC STANDARD I

A school administrator is an educational leader who promotes the success of all students by facilitating the development, articulation, implementation, and stewardship of a vision of learning that is shared and supported by the school community.

This standard is key to the community's overall perception of the school district. Virtually every mission statement written by school districts cites the belief that *every* student can and will be successful. Clearly this goal is admirable and necessary in the world of public education. In spite of this written mission statement, some schools do not *operate* as though they believe *all* students can learn, and many administrators do not make individual decisions that support this belief. For instance, many schools across the country have graduation rates at or near 50 percent. As important as this standard is for student success, many districts still function as Darwinian experiences with only the most capable and dedicated students surviving.

As a result, there are some vital characteristics, beliefs, and actions of the administrator exhibiting the traits illustrated by ISLLC standard 1. The successful administrators have knowledge in systems theory and the principles of developing and implementing strategic plans, and are committed to continuous school improvement. They must also be effective communicators. It is clearly not sufficient for the administrators to have only these core beliefs; they must also be able to collaboratively work with all staff, students, and community members to build consensus for achieving the necessary means for the success of all students.

In examining ISLLC standard 1, it is important to discuss the relevance of data collection, analysis, and how this information relates to the overall school improvement process. The principal must strive to ensure that this information is communicated to all stakeholders. The principal is skilled at examining the barriers that may impede the school improvement process. Further, a successful principal understands the relevant demographic data of the students and their families in the community.

Although there is a place for gut reactions and quick thinking in the administrative ranks, one should not rely on these skills for long-term goals and projects requiring district resources. Further, ideal school leaders realize it is not possible to have all the answers in every scenario and are willing to utilize the human resources at their disposal. Instructional leaders should have a willingness to seek input from all stakeholders and understand that knowledge of the community, student performance, and a strong vision is built on a foundation of data that supports leadership decisions.

Lastly, the successful principal realizes situations, demographics, and stakeholders change over time. The vision or mission of the district should be continually monitored, evaluated, and revised. In addition, a successful administrator is willing to continually examine his or her own assumptions, beliefs, and practices.

ISLLC STANDARD 2

A school administrator is an educational leader who promotes the success of all students by advocating, nurturing, and sustaining a school culture and instructional program conducive to student learning and staff professional growth.

While ISLLC standard 1 dealt with the need for strong vision and the skills necessary for implementation of that vision, ISLLC standard 2 relates to knowledge of student learning and the teaching process. An educational leader *must* have an in-depth knowledge of pedagogy and a thorough understanding of how students learn and develop. While the skills necessary for school change are important, it is equally important to understand the learning and teaching processes. Indeed, standards 1 and 2 should be intertwined; the vision of the district should address student learning and the strengths and weaknesses of the district in addressing barriers to this process.

A successful instructional leader should have the ability to affect or change the culture of the building or district in question. Student learning/achievement should be the primary goal of all discussions, meetings, professional growth, and communication. It should be readily apparent to *all* stakeholders the emphasis the administration places on student learning.

A principal skilled in standard 2 understands that all students should be treated fairly with dignity and respect. Students must feel valued and respected if learning is to take place. Further, motivational theories must be utilized when students are not successful, and programs should be designed with student needs in mind to eliminate many of the barriers prohibiting the learning process.

In designing coherent, effective curricular and cocurricular activities, it is also important to remember the roles of diversity and technology for student success. Not all students are the same and cultural influences are ever-present in the public school setting. If the school setting is nurturing and caring, students and their families are more likely to feel welcomed and valued. Further, technological skills are increasingly important in today's world, and students must have adequate preparation if they are to have the proper foundation for success in a global economy.

It is equally important that staff members feel valued and respected. Staff development is vital in the school improvement process, and a disenfranchised staff is less likely to actively participate in school improvement initiatives or activities that model lifelong learning. Resources and professional development must be available to the staff if an attitude of growth or improvement is to be maintained.

A successful school culture perpetually embraces student and staff growth and achievement. Student and staff achievements are celebrated and recognized. The successful administrator never misses an opportunity to point out achievement and understands that success breeds success in an accomplished school climate.

ISLLC STANDARD 3

A school administrator is an educational leader who promotes the success of all students by ensuring management of the organization, operations, and resources for a safe, efficient, and effective learning environment.

Students and staff must feel safe, secure and comfortable if learning is to take place.

This standard incorporates a wide range of items from school violence to school utilities. Often it is the *assistant* principal's role that is vital to the administration's success in addressing standard 3. It is often the assistant principal who is the first administrator addressing these day-to-day discipline issues and "fires" that arise throughout the day.

Discipline issues are directly related to this standard. It is vital the administration has a thorough understanding of board policy related to student behavior. Also, the principal must be able to utilize school resources for the success of all students, even those who may adversely affect the learning of others. Simple disposal of problem students is not the answer. Discipline issues must be addressed in a firm, consistent, and swift fashion to avoid chaos, but the educational mandate to teach *all* students still must be met.

The learning environment is not simply dealing with and addressing problem students. The school climate also is affected by simple things such as the temperature, lighting, or cleanliness of the building and grounds. The administrator who exhibits success with standard 3 understands the importance of operational procedures at the school and district levels. Further, he/she works to align human, financial, and material resources with the goals and vision of the district and maintains accurate records of day-to-day operations of the building.

Establishing a successful learning environment also involves the ability to effectively manage personnel issues. To do this, the administration must understand the importance of hiring practices and the collective bargaining agreement, as quality personnel will reduce the need for administrative assistance.

Last, an effective school leader exhibits skill in this area by trusting others' ideas and opinions. This individual is willing to take risks, involve stakeholders in decision making, and accept responsibilities for decisions involving the learning environment.

ISLLC STANDARD 4

A school administrator is an educational leader who promotes the success of all students by collaborating with families and community members, responding to diverse community interests and needs, and mobilizing community resources.

This standard deals with the administrator's knowledge of the school community. It is not realistic to expect an administrator to take a position in a new community and immediately have the expertise necessary for mastery in ISLLC standard 4. However, a new administrator must continually strive to gain this valuable insight.

ISLLC standard 4 addresses a need for administrative personnel to cultivate relationships with families and involve them in decision-making processes. The view should be taken that the family is a resource in the education of children and *most* families have the best interest of their children in mind regarding education. The administration should model this behavior and have the same expectations of all staff. If teachers are to be successful, the community must be involved in the teaching process. The most successful schools are an integral part of the larger community, and an informed, involved public assists in this process.

Second, several areas must be studied when examining the community demographics. First, closely examine the diversity of the school environment and examine how this diversity affects the learning culture and the resources available to the building. Further, perpetually question the models of school, family, government agency, and business partnerships that exist. Diversity should be celebrated and honored, further encouraging communication with all stakeholders involved in the learning process.

Last, ISLLC standard 4 encourages the principal or assistant principal to recognize valuable resources within the community. A wise school administrator realizes the school does not exist in a vacuum and will put energy and effort into maintaining and cultivating new partnerships. A successful administrator is active and, most important, *visible* in community events and functions. The community should feel as though the administrators are approachable in the school setting and truly value their input.

ISLLC STANDARD 5

A school administrator is an educational leader who promotes the success of all students by acting with integrity, fairness, and in an ethical manner.

ISLLC standard 5 is best defined as the examination of the character exhibited by the leader of the school or district. The successful administrator can complete job duties involving students, positively or negatively, and still be viewed as *consistent* and *fair*. It is a never-ending complaint by many of the students in many schools across the country: the administration plays favorites. All students *should* feel as though the administration has their best interest at heart, even if a decision is made that might adversely affect the student at that moment.

Character is not only important when dealing with students, but it is equally important when dealing with staff. Honesty and integrity are vital when involving all staff regardless of job description. If school personnel believe the administration cannot be trusted, "buy-in" cannot exist when completing school improvement initiatives. All staff will have varying strengths and weaknesses, but all staff should be valued for the worth they bring to the district. Successful principals should expect to see this respect shown from staff when they address students in their individual classrooms; therefore, modeling this behavior is vital to the success of the building.

The district should also develop a code of ethics that outlines the expectations of the administrators in the district. This process should involve input from all stakeholders in the learning process, and the expectations may extend beyond the normal hours in the school setting. Entry-year administrators should develop a thorough understanding of the expectations of the state in which they reside, the board of education, and the school community.

If one is to exhibit mastery of this standard, the principal should understand the role of education in its historical context and operate with the belief that education exists for the common good of society. All students should be afforded a free, quality, and nurturing education. Administrators should act as servant leaders who are capable of subordinating their own interests for the greater good of the school community. This role model approach to education can be difficult to achieve, but it should be an ever-present characteristic in the management style of the successful principal.

ISLLC STANDARD 6

A school administrator is an educational leader who promotes the success of all students by understanding, responding to, and influencing the larger political, social, economic, legal, and cultural context.

Education can, at times, operate on a pendulum. Public opinion, media coverage, court rulings, and government legislation all affect the manner in which this pendulum sways. The wise, effective, knowledgeable administrator understands the impact these groups have on the operations of the district. Further, depending on the location of your current working situation, world issues such as economic trends and federal international policy can all affect day-to-day operations.

The successful principal realizes media coverage of school violence, current employment trends, and economic issues will stir public interest in education. Education has long been viewed as the cure of many of the ills of society, and politicians have often noted the need for quality schools at election time. As a result of this constant barrage of coverage, schools are (and always will be) under the microscope of public scrutiny. ISLLC standard 6 requires that the principal understands these societal pressures and follows the current trends affecting public schooling.

Further, court rulings constantly change school handbooks, board policy, and administrative guidelines. The administrator exhibiting efficiency in regards to standard six understands this and attempts to follow and anticipate recent educational legal trends. While it is never advisable for schools to fear impending lawsuits and litigation, it is advisable to understand the vast resources that could be squandered defending an uninformed decision by an entry-year administrator.

Lastly, one would only need to examine the impact of technology on the education system to fully understand the need for the principal to follow larger societal and cultural issues when becoming an educational leader. Technology has changed the method in which we communicate with one another, gain information, and deliver the necessary curriculum to students. Indeed, there are various other global issues that constantly affect teaching and learning; it is imperative administrative personnel understand these forces and realize the role education plays in student opportunity and social mobility.

Overall, the standards are widely disseminated and accepted as a good source for the direction of many school improvement initiatives and professional development in the educational administrative profession. Further, without a guide or reference point, any professional growth will be inhibited and the six standards adopted will serve as the starting point for this growth process.

As stated previously, the focus of the assistant principal can be very narrow and not provide the opportunity to delve deeply into all six standards adopted by the coalition. As you continue with the reading, you will find the great majority of the assistant principal administrative duties fall under ISLLC standards 2, 3, and 5. Further, many topics, duties, or tasks may apply to more than one standard and this could cause some confusion. The point is to not get bogged down by the semantics, but rather to address the topics in preparation for a successful first year and become acquainted with the standards for future dialogue with professional colleagues.

The six standards to be outlined with the knowledge, dispositions, and performance indicators and the CCSSO can be researched further by visiting the following web site: http://www.ccsso.org and searching for the *ISLLC Standards for School Leaders*.

NOTE

1. Council of Chief State School Officers. (1996). Interstate School Leaders Licensure Consortium (ISLLC) Standards for School Leaders. Washington, DC: Author. Available: http://www.ccsso.org/content/pdfs/isllcstd.pdf. The Interstate School Leaders Licensure Consortium (ISLLC) Standards for School Leaders (Council of Chief State School Officers, 1996) were written by representatives from states and professional associations in a partnership with the National Policy Board for Educational Administration in 1994–1995, supported by grants from the Pew Charitable Trusts and the Danforth Foundation. The standards were published by the Council of Chief State School Officers, copyright © 1996 and are currently being updated.

2

UNDERSTANDING YOUR ROLE

Once you have reviewed the ISLLC Standards for School Leaders, it should be apparent that certain issues and responsibilities are clearly under the role of the principal of the school building. The principal will have the authority to exercise control over *most* of the day-to-day issues that arise in the school setting. Also, his/her personality will dictate just how much control will be delegated to you as the assistant principal. Further, the age of the students may have a bearing on the role of the assistant principal. For instance, if the position is at the elementary level, less time may be devoted to discipline; whereas, the high school assistant may spend an enormous amount of time disciplining the student population.

Even though the scope appears narrow, the importance of the *assistant* principal's position cannot be overstated; it is the principal who will set the tone for the building, but the assistant principal is the individual who, inevitably, sets the tone for discipline. He/she will be viewed as the police officer in the office. The assistant principal will conduct investigations, question students, and be the first to initiate the discipline process and ensure the handbook and the school dress code are enforced according to board policy.

Whatever the situation, it is vital that there is *open and thorough* communication between the principal and the assistant(s). A meeting should take place well before the hustle and bustle of the first days of school to determine exactly who is responsible for specific job duties and to discuss the principal's view of the assistant's role in the day-to-day operations of the school. If the principal does not initiate this meeting, you should request the opportunity to address the roles and responsibilities for the upcoming school year.

The following questions should be discussed in a beginning of the year meeting with the building principal. Sample answers are provided that are generally desirable for the entry-year administrator's growth, but it should be understood that each administrative position is different. Therefore, due to variables such as size of the district, grade level, personality of the principal, location of the school (state and/or city), and board policy, it is impossible to predict all possible responses to the following questions.

What function does the assistant principal play in the overall instructional programs in the building?

Initially, it is not advisable for any first-year administrator to make large sweeping changes to instructional programs. The first year should be a learning experience and a time for data collection. However, if you possess expertise in a certain area, (standardized testing, for instance) you may want to include this in your discussion of the upcoming year's activities.

At what point should I bring you into a discipline situation?

Most principals would want to be informed of any situation that involves a suspension from school or a change to the learning environment. At the beginning of the year, it would be advisable to arrange time for daily interaction to rehash the day's events. In this manner, you may deal with issues as they arise and still keep your supervisor informed. You should keep in mind, a parent may wish to meet with the principal at a later time regarding an issue you handled.

Do I have a role in the planning of staff development? If so, what is that role?

If you are fortunate, you may have a role in this process. It is important for staff to see you as an instructional leader and this is an opportunity for you to fulfill this role. Some principals go to great lengths in planning and organizing staff development and in-service opportunities; others find these days cumbersome and tedious. Hopefully, your supervisor understands the need and benefits from such moments and allows the assistant to participate in such measures.

Are there current district issues that need addressing on which I need to be brought up to speed?

Answers here will vary. If there are, make certain to ask for all history regarding this issue. If not, be certain to question the principal's school improvement agenda and discuss your role in completion of any immediate tasks.

Are there major projects or events that I am to oversee for which I can begin preparations at this time?

Again, answers may vary. The entry-year administrator may be arriving at a time when there are no major events or activities on the docket. Most principals fulfilled the role of assistant before promotion to their current position. As a result, they can provide guidance with any activities that are large in scope or community involvement.

What extra duties or extra-curricular events do I need to cover and assume the administrative role?

Many assistant principals will find themselves covering athletic events, musical functions, or after-school meetings—especially for the secondary level administration. It is important to be fully aware of this *before* entering the position and expect to work many hours beyond the school day. These events could have an impact on family and other activities in which you may be involved. Allowing the principal to understand other commitments limiting your availability reduces the opportunity for problems later in the school year.

What is my role in the observation or evaluation of staff members?
What evaluation instrument is the district currently utilizing?
The evaluation of staff provides a further opportunity to be viewed as an instructional leader and not merely the handbook enforcer. If you are fortunate to be permitted to participate in this process, take advantage of this opportunity. However, if a staff member is facing nonrenewal, it is advisable for the entry-year administrator to have oversight in this process.

What are your expectations for me during my first year in the role of assistant principal?
Answers will vary, but the best entry-year experience will call for collegial and close-knit opportunities for success. As stated previously, the initial year is a learning process, but professional growth will be directly related to the expectations of the principal and the experiences in which the assistant is allowed to participate.

Will I be involved in the disciplining or reprimanding of staff? If so, how?
Many districts expect the principal to fulfill this role. However, a negative position to be put in is the place of "tattletale," in which you are expected to report any negative behavior, and then be set aside while the principal addresses *your* concerns. To avoid this, one suggestion is to, at least, be present when it is necessary to address any personnel with concerns that arise during the completion of your job duties.

Is there sufficient time or funding available for my own professional development?
The first year in administration is survival, much like that of the entry-year teacher. There should always be moments and re-

sources for professional growth of all personnel, and this definitely includes the administration. If there are no resources available, continue to seek other avenues and continue to address your growth. Modeling this behavior is important if you expect this from your teaching staff.

Are there opportunities for the assistant and the principal to meet regularly throughout the year for the purposes of dialogue and communication?

Ideally, the principal should assume a mentoring role and facilitate these meetings. There should be time regularly scheduled for this purpose. If there is not, it is strongly recommended you request such opportunities. Clear communication will only assist in the entry-year assistant's smooth transition in the administrative ranks.

How will I be formally and informally evaluated in my duties? By whom?

If you are only given a one-year contract in your first position, this is an especially important question. Further, you should know *initially* what the expectations are and what administrative instrument will be utilized in your evaluation. Typically, many administrative evaluation tools involve goal setting as the basis for a successful term, and this may be quite different from the tools utilized to measure teacher performance. Also, evaluation timelines are important and should be addressed as well.

How much authority do I possess in dealing with staff and curricular issues?

Never confuse *positional authority* with respect and credibility from the staff. Most staff members do not respect an *administrative position* as much as the *administrator!* The entry-year administrator should not assume they have *power* to control all aspects of the school setting simply due to the entrance in an administrative position. Remember, the first year is a learning and growing experience and should be treated as such. However, some staff members may attempt to take advantage of the rookie, and no administrator should be disrespected merely due to inexperience.

Will I have the opportunity/responsibility to speak at staff meetings and address the staff? Are there committees which I could lead/chair?

As an assistant principal, if you wish to be more than the school's "enforcement officer," these moments are invaluable in the image the entry-year administrator will portray. These are the very occasions when the respect from the staff can be fostered. Take advantage of any opportunity given and perpetually request the opportunity to address staff regardless of how trivial the issue may be. One should never shy away from leadership positions or opportunities. Also keep in mind, the assistant principal position is preparation for higher ranks; be certain to utilize it as a learning and growth opportunity.

What is the proper policy or steps for the search of a student or his/her locker? What is board policy if the police wish to question a student regarding an incident?

There are clear federal/state laws regarding such issues, and they can vary from location to location. It is imperative you understand these policies and laws *before* you are involved in a situation requiring such searches or police questioning. It is advisable to involve the principal during an initial search of any student's locker or belongings—especially if the student is of the opposite gender!

Is there a job description for the assistant principal position?

Most districts have a job description for all positions in the district. It is advisable to have this available as you continue this discussion. (If one is not available or present, a strong recommendation is to work with your mentor/supervisor in developing one for future use.)

To further illustrate the difficulties in defining the assistant principal position and discover how the position can change from district to district, I have included a sample job description for review purposes (see figure 2.1). Compare the following assistant principal job description from the Northeastern Local School District near Springfield, Ohio, to that of your own district, and be prepared to answer the questions that follow.

Careful review of the job description provided illustrates the impossible task of attempting to list all duties or expectations of the assistant principal position. As a result, many districts will have a disclaimer statement that gives the principal or superintendent the ability to add/delete tasks assigned to the assistant's position. The Northeastern assistant principal description provided has three such statements highlighted and provides an example of disclaimer statements and how they can be utilized in employment position descriptions.

As you compare the previous description of the assistant principal to the description in your own district with your mentor, discuss the following questions:

1. What similarities are present between your district job description and the provided sample job description?
2. Are there noticeable differences between the two job descriptions?
3. Which ISLLC standards would best correlate with the duties described in the sample job description? In your job description?
4. Does your district description contain a disclaimer statement? If so, are the statements similar to those highlighted in the Northeastern Assistant Principal Description?

Northeastern Local Schools
Board of Education
Job Description

Title:	2.02 Assistant Principal
Reports to:	Principal, Local Superintendent
Employment Status:	Full Time
FLSA Status:	Exempt
Qualifications:	1. State of Ohio Principal's Certificate/License
	2. Valid Driver's License
General Description:	1. To cooperatively work with the principal in the maintenance of appropriate instructional and extra curricular programs for the benefit of students.
	2. To assist the principal by carrying out designated duties in directing the daily activities of the staff and students.
	3. Shall act in the capacity of the principal during his/her absence from duty. The assistant principal shall become familiar with all phases of the school program.

Essential Functions:

1. Shall assist with securing board approved substitute teachers and help them to become familiar with their duties and with school procedures.
2. Supervises pupil attendance, keeping accurate records, issuing permits, checking with parents, and referring problem cases to Juvenile Court.
3. Controls all but the most serious discipline problems and confers with the student's teachers, parents, and counselors to bring about needed adjustments.
4. Directs distribution of grade cards to students with copies of grades to homeroom teachers and counselors; helps counsel those students with failing grades; sets up conferences with students, teachers, counselors and parent/guardians.
5. Assists in the admission, assignment, and withdrawal of students. Refers withdrawing students to counselors for final review.
6. Assumes responsibility for record keeping. This includes the opportunity to become familiar with the school activity account.
7. Supervises requisitions and distributes classroom and office supplies, textbooks, and equipment.
8. Helps maintain order in the halls during the school day, during class changes, at fire drills, assemblies, and so forth.
9. Assists with maintaining records of teacher attendance, absence and so forth.
10. *Accepts and performs the delegated responsibilities assigned by the principal.*
11. Attends school functions, curricular, extra-curricular activities, and athletic activities, as often as possible or as requested by the principal.

12. Assumes the responsibility of acting principal in the absence of the principal.
13. Works with the principal in the evaluation of building personnel.
14. Completes building, local, county, state, and federal reports as assigned by the principal.

Other Duties and Responsibilities:
1. Serves as a role model for students in how to conduct themselves as citizens and as responsible, intelligent human beings.
2. Helps instill in students the belief in and practice of ethical principles and democratic values; and
3. *Conducts other duties related to the assistant principal's duties as assigned by the principal or local superintendent.*

Additional Working Conditions:
1. Occasional exposure to blood, bodily fluids, and tissue.
2. Occasional operation of a vehicle under inclement weather conditions.
3. Occasional interaction with unruly children.

Title: 2.02   Assistant Principal

This job description in no manner states or implies that these are the only duties and responsibilities to be performed by the position incumbent. The incumbent will be required to follow the instruction and perform the duties required by the incumbent's supervisor, appointing authority or designee.

_____   _____
Superintendent of designee   Date

My signature below signifies I have received the contents of my job description and that I am aware of the requirements of my position. I further certify that I have reviewed the most current copy of the Northeastern Local Board of Education Policy Manual.

_____   _____
Superintendent of designee   Date

Figure 2.1.   Northeastern Local Schools Board of Education Job Description

After working through these exercises, you will undoubtedly realize the necessity for the limited focus of the assistant principal's position. Imagine the confusion by the staff and the student population if there were not a clear designation of responsibility and chain of command. Further, you will need and *want* to have a thorough knowledge of your role in the building. This knowledge provides for a clear understanding by the students and staff and also prevents any impression that you are intruding on areas outside your job description and attempting to undermine the principal. The relationship between the assistant and the principal is paramount for sound leadership; having clearly defined roles only aids in this process.

3

PROFESSIONAL GROWTH

In addition to the daily dealings with students and staff, there will be opportunities for growth throughout the school year. As mentioned in an earlier chapter, assigning a mentor to the first-year assistant principal can be invaluable. Many states are adopting programs for entry-year positions, and it is probable that you will be required to participate in such a process. Due to availability and "population pool size," the mentor may be *assigned* to the entry-year administrator. Sometimes, by chance, an assigned mentorship can prove very beneficial and foster valuable growth in the new administrator.

In other cases, however, the success of the program is measured by mere completion, not by improvements made. Therefore, if the assistant has the opportunity to choose the individual to work with and grow professionally, there may be a much greater opportunity for *true* professional growth. If you are fortunate enough to be able to select your mentor, the following are qualities on which to focus as you make your selection.

First and foremost, the person assuming the mentoring role must *want* to do so. If the mentoring role is thrust on an individual, he/she is much less likely to be effective or motivated to see the success of the new administrator. The mentor should appreciate the value of this experience and be willing to put forth the time and effort required for successful completion.

Second, the mentor should be knowledgeable with some administrative experience. It will truly be the "blind leading the blind" if the mentor is in the first or second year of administration in the position or district. Remember, one of the goals of the program should be the shortening of the learning curve. There is no replacing the benefits that can be garnered by conversing with a seasoned veteran accustomed to dealing with your new position.

Next, the mentor must have the time, opportunity, and resources necessary to work with the new administrator. Often, the best of intentions fall short due to minimal resources and time. The fact that a mentor *wants* to assist does not always guarantee that they are *able* to help. The necessity for ample time for regular meetings to take place between the entry-year administrator and the veteran administrator cannot be understated.

If at all possible, an effort should be made to match the new administrator with an individual who is *not* responsible for evaluation purposes. The best programs allow for dialogue to express frustrations and questions, and solicit advice for dealing with difficult issues. The assistant principal may not feel comfortable seeking such advice if he/she believes it could ultimately be used as a shortcoming in a future evaluation tool.

Lastly, *trust* must be present between the individuals in this mentoring process. Many conversations may be confidential, and an open dialogue is paramount in a successful mentoring program. The entry-year administrator may meet the mentor for the first time and initially there could be little trust or dialogue. This is to be expected, but over time, with regular and organized meetings taking place a positive rapport can be established.

ACTIVITIES FOR THE FIRST-YEAR ADMINISTRATOR

This section focuses on those activities that will aid you in your development as an assistant principal and assist in the preparation of those individuals desiring to move into the role of principal. Many of the following activities are designed to give the assistant principal a broader role and a better foundation for future positions.

1. Conduct (at least) one staff meeting.

This will enable the staff to see the entry-year administrator in a leadership position. It would be even more beneficial if you were able to lead a study group discussion, an orientation of new teachers to the district, or one session of a staff development/in-service day. Any time the entry year administrator is placed in a leadership position, it aids in the development process and builds confidence. Further, these activities could be the deciding factor in an interview process, if another district is looking for experience from their potential instructional leader. Remember to consider the principal's attitudes toward the role of the assistant principal before attempting to assume a larger leadership role!

2. Conduct (at least) two staff evaluations.

Some principals are reluctant to allow entry-year administrators to complete the evaluations of personnel for employment purposes. If you find yourself in this situation, it may be helpful to sit in with the principal and complete a mock evaluation. This will allow both administrators to compare notes and give you the opportunity to see just how efficient you would be if it were an actual district requirement. For these purposes, two evaluations are recommended as this allows for the assistant administrator to evaluate not only a certified staff member, but a classified staff member as well.

3. Attend two board of education meetings.

Most administrators are required to attend and give building progress reports regularly at board meetings. If this is the case in your district, be willing to observe your principal or colleague fulfilling this role. If the principal is willing to relinquish this duty for one evening, it may be beneficial for the assistant principal to fill in and gain from the experience.

4. Assist in the management/distribution/mailing of standardized proficiency or achievement testing.

This can be a tedious and cumbersome job. If this is not currently a task for the assistant principal, the individual assigned this task (usually a guidance counselor or test coordinator) may appreciate the assistance. There are undoubtedly specific rules and regulations for the security and distribution of these materials. Performing these tasks will not only allow the entry-year administrator the opportunity to learn those procedures, it will also provide an opportunity to gain an appreciation for the behind-the-scenes work that is needed to conduct such an important state mandate.

5. Conduct or take part in (at least) two special education/IEP meetings.

These are annual events which usually take a large amount of time in the spring of the year. Some of the meetings can be very lengthy and costly to the district if unnecessary decisions are made. Conversely, students can be left high and dry if they are not properly represented at these important functions. Again, it may be a requirement for the assistant principal to assume some responsibility in this arena, but if it is not, the opportunity for growth is vital to those individuals wishing to become promoted in the administrative ranks.

6. Attend (at least) two end-of-the-year banquets or awards ceremonies.

These are numerous and come at the busiest time of the year for many administrators. Just as the year is winding down and the paperwork is mounting, virtually every evening is filled with some sort of banquet honoring student achievement. Attending these functions is good preparation for a future principal's position, but it also serves as a community relations tool for parents and students to see the assistant principal do more than just discipline. Never shy away from an opportunity to show appreciation for student achievement and to build positive student/administrator interaction.

7. Become involved in the school improvement process.

Every principal must be able to demonstrate leadership and vision for the building and/or district. If the assistant principal is to move forward in his/her career, he/she must be able to demonstrate an understanding of the school improvement process (IS-LLC standard 1). The entry-year administrator must take an active role in some improvement initiatives such as the building's North Central Accreditation process, the state's continuous improvement process, or a "schools that work" initiative. Although this is not a typical duty or task of the entry-year *assistant* principal, an understanding of these programs is paramount if you are willing to make the commitment to be a successful administrator.

8. Create a record for desired changes.

Part of demonstrating good leadership skills is the ability to evaluate and improve existing policies and programs. As the year progresses, a quality administrator will reflect on the year and reevaluate the situations and decisions that were made. Then, throughout the year, a folder, document, or file should be maintained to record the necessary changes to existing policy. This allows for greater student achievement (ISLLC standard 2), better communication with community (ISLLC standard 4), and possibly better efficiency from the administrative staff (ISLLC standard 3).

9. *Take a leadership role in community events.*

Just as it is important for the faculty and staff to see the new assistant as a leader, it is equally important for the community to recognize the assistant principal and see that individual's leadership qualities. The following tasks precipitate visibility: supervising sporting events, speaking to incoming parents during some type of orientation to the building (kindergarten or freshmen, for example), or volunteering to assist with a levy campaign if the district is involved in this process. Activities such as these provide both the opportunity for community support, as well as an opportunity to showcase the leadership qualities that led to your decision to join the administrative ranks.

10. *Work closely with some student organization.*

As previously discussed, it is vital for assistant principals to expand their duties. The entry-year administrator cannot miss an opportunity to work with students in a positive setting. Suggestions include working with a student council for a fund-raising activity, working with the school's chapter of the National Honor Society or the National Junior Honor Society in some worthwhile project, or assisting with a student-led initiative supporting a worthy cause.

11. *Become familiar with necessary technologies.*

As students become more skilled at cheating and utilizing technology in negative ways, the assistant principal should attempt to keep up with some of the latest hardware, software, and web sites utilized by the student population. Students have become very adept at cheating on research papers, sending texts of assessment pieces to classmates, or electronically bullying/hazing classmates via the Internet. Again, it is the assistant who will deal with most discipline situations, and in today's environment, technology will almost certainly play a role in many of the issues that arise in the school environment.

There are also several computer programs with which you will almost certainly become quickly acquainted as you move through the administrative ranks. Undoubtedly, you have taken many college courses and had to become more than competent in utilizing word processing programs. As you will soon discover, the need to document is a certainty, and this skill will serve you well as you progress in the administrative ranks. Further, electronic mail is now the norm, and staff will expect competence in this area.

Further, the need to utilize spreadsheet information will also be necessary. More and more student testing is converted to spreadsheet form for teachers to measure benchmarks and track student progress. Often, the administration is assigned the task of breaking down raw data and conducting in-services on the usefulness of such information to the individual classroom teacher.

Lastly, as presentation to staff and the community is an essential portion of administrative duties, an understanding of presentation software such as PowerPoint is almost a necessity. You will find yourself in front of rooms of individuals, and a well-done visual presentation can be a powerful teaching tool in these situations—even for adults.

These eleven activities will be beneficial to the assistant principal in a number of ways. First, the students will work closely with you in a positive setting and relationships can be cultivated. Second, the activities will improve the morale of the entry-year administrator. While working with at-risk students can be rewarding, it can also be exhausting and the opportunity to work with the district's best can be very enjoyable and jump start your momentum. Finally, the community relations' benefit that stems from these projects can only assist in building a lasting impression for you in your entry year.

ACTIVITIES FOR THE ENTRY-YEAR ADMINISTRATOR'S MENTOR

The most important task for the mentor is to act in a supportive role. The assistant may become overwhelmed with all of the pressure that arrives with assuming one's first administrative position. It is vital to maintain a quality relationship with positive, open lines of communication. One should remember the mentoring process could be equally as important and beneficial to the mentor as to the entry-year administrator. The following is meant to provide activities to improve this process.

1. Open the communication.

There should be regular meetings scheduled, in advance, that allow for perpetual communication between the parties. The mentor should be available for impromptu meetings as well, allowing the assistant to seek advice or a sounding board for an important issue. These moments should not replace the more relaxed discussions that should take place regularly throughout the year. A strong suggestion is for the mentor to initiate the contact between the parties and meet on the assistant principal's turf. This may make the entry-year administrator more comfortable and less intimidated discussing issues relevant to the position.

2. Provide written goals for the mentoring process.

The new administrator may be forced to attend these mentoring functions to meet a state or district mandate. This pressure may initially hinder the mentoring relationship. Both parties must understand and be open-minded regarding the professional development that occurs during this process. By providing written documentation of the goals and outcomes, the mentoring situation begins more successfully and the parties can agree on the mutual benefits that can be attained.

3. Discuss the scenarios throughout the entry-year manual.

During your annual meetings with the entry-year administrator, take a moment to discuss the scenarios presented throughout the manual. The scenarios provided are taken from personal experience and the opportunity to engage in nonpressure situations will better prepare the assistant principal should an actual event take place. All administrators become more skilled with life experience. While there is no substitute for this experience, the discussions precipitated by the entry-year manual will provide some foundation for future events.

4. Provide networking contacts for unanswered questions.
No one expects the mentor to have all the answers. In fact, in the world of public school administration, the issues are so varied, it would be virtually impossible for anyone to have the answers to all the questions that will arise for the first-year administrator. The best administrators realize this and have a network of contacts who can provide needed information that is not readily available to them. Sharing these contacts and assisting the beginning administrator in building his/her own contacts may be the most important tool provided during the mentoring process.

5. Review the ISLLC standards and the methods the entry-year administrator can use to show evidence of meeting those standards.
It is important for the mentor to understand the enormous amount of time, dedication, and work necessary to survive the first year of administration. The mentoring process is *not* meant to add stress, hours, or work for an already busy schedule. The most valuable role a mentor can serve for the assistant principal is that of an advisor who can provide guidance for the entry-year administrator.

It is best not to treat the following information on the standards as a checklist required to successfully complete a mentor program. The administrator's future years will be ample time for portfolio development. Rather, the purpose of this section is to assist in understanding the assistant principal's position and techniques to aid in a successful first year of administration. The following lists are taken from Fred Lindley's *The Portable Mentor* and are provided as another discussion topic for the mentor/entry-year administrator relationship.

List #1

Examples of artifacts that validate the principal's leadership in activities related to ISLLC standard 1.

ISLLC standard 1: A school administrator is an educational leader who promotes the success of all students by facilitating the development, articulation, implementation, and stewardship of a vision of learning that is shared and supported by the community.

- a copy of the school's mission statement or photographs of the posted mission statement
- a copy of sections of the school's continuous improvement plan
- a copy of posted rules, expectations, and goals
- samples of agendas, minutes, and membership lists of committees
- copies of grant applications
- a copy of the building "report card"
- a copy of the school's strategic plan
- samples of the school newsletter; printouts of the school's website
- copies of community survey instrument(s); results from surveys
- pictures of the school's marquee (various messages)

List #2

Examples of artifacts that validate the principal's leadership in activities related to ISLLC standard 2.

ISLLC standard 2: A school administrator is an educational leader who promotes the success of all students by advocating, nurturing, and sustaining a school culture and instructional program conducive to student learning and staff professional growth.

- records of student test scores that reflect improvement
- documents that verify the provision of programs to improve student performance
- schedules of classes and other records that display inclusionary practices
- documents that verify the existence of recognition programs
- lists of rewards given to students who demonstrate desirable behavior
- documents that verify the existence of conflict resolution programs
- records of student and staff involvement in decision making
- records that verify that teachers plan and deliver learning activities in a variety of teaching styles to accommodate the various learning styles of the students
- records that show staff and principal participation in professional development activities (building, district, and beyond)
- documents that display instructional leadership (memo, articles shared, conferences attended, and initiatives supported)

List #3

Examples of artifacts that validate the principal's leadership in activities related to ISLLC standard 3.

ISLLC standard 3: A school administrator is an educational leader who promotes the success of all students by ensuring management of the organization, operations, and resources for a safe, efficient, and effective learning environment.

- copies or sections of handbooks—student, parent, staff, volunteers
- survey results that reflect feelings of staff, students, and community about safety and academic progress
- records that verify staff, student, and parent representation in the operation of the school, including a problem-solving system

- records that display scheduled, internal audits of the work environment
- records of communication to all school stakeholders and staff that enhance school organization (building schedules, daily bulletins, reminder memos, calendars regarding upcoming events and dates)
- documents that display an active parent-teacher organization (agendas and minutes of meetings, budget statements, newsletters)
- records that display a proactive and positive public relations effort toward the community (parent-teacher organization, newsletters, flyers, website, telephone hotline, committees, open houses, outreach programs)

List #4

Examples of artifacts that validate the principal's leadership in activities related to ISLLC standard 4.

ISLLC standard 4: A school administrator is an educational leader who promotes the success of all students by collaborating with families and community members, responding to diverse community interests and needs, and maintaining community resources.

- records verifying student community service and volunteer programs
- records that display performance programs within the community
- printed programs associated with events that promote diversity
- evidence of students' participation in diversity activities (plays, workshops)
- records that display staff involvement at community events
- records verifying staff involvement in community clubs, groups, and projects

- records that display the school's efforts to access and use the talents of community members as resource speakers
- records that display the existence and proactive use of a diverse, broad-based principal's advisory committee
- records that verify the involvement of community members in curriculum review or revision

List #5

Examples of artifacts that validate the principal's leadership in activities related to ISLLC standard 5.

ISLLC standard 5: A school administrator is an educational leader who promotes the success of all students by acting with integrity, fairness, and in an ethical manner.

- records that confirm and display the use of a conflict resolution process
- records of surveys that confirm student satisfaction with fair and ethical treatment and their involvement in decision making
- copies of the school's mission statement that express an expectation that all staff members act with integrity and fairness, and in an ethical manner
- records of survey instruments and survey results that confirm community, student, and staff satisfaction with the ethical environment and atmosphere at the school
- records of internal audits that confirm the curriculum is equitable, diverse, and multicultural
- records that display the regular use of a process for community input
- survey instruments and results that display the community's satisfaction with the ethics and fairness of the principal's decisions and actions

- records that verify the regularly scheduled celebration of diversity through holidays, events, and celebrations

List #6

Examples of artifacts that validate the principal's leadership in activities related to ISLLC standard 6.

ISLLC standard 6: A school administrator is an educational leader who promotes the success of all students by understanding, responding to, and influencing the larger political, social, economic, legal, and cultural context.

- records that verify a planned effort by school leadership to keep the community informed and updated on state and federal initiatives, regulations, and standards
- records that verify the involvement of the principal in educational and community organizations
- evidence of programs related to global issues
- evidence of citizen education programs
- notes and summaries from labor-management meetings.
- evidence of efforts to monitor and influence school-related legislation
- notes and summaries from parent and community advisory committee meetings
- records that confirm community representatives serve on building or district committees for short- and long-range planning and goal-setting forums
- documents that confirm community involvement in curriculum review, revision, or adoption

4

LEARN TO DOCUMENT
CONVERSATIONS

Good administrators, regardless of the level and position, document regularly and precisely. At times, the need to do so may seem cumbersome, monotonous, and tedious, but any administrator who has been required to attend an appeal hearing weeks after an issue was discussed will underscore the importance of taking copious notes. I summarize note taking in this manner: If you speak with a parent in the office or on the telephone, document the conversation. If you speak with a student, document the conversation. If you speak with a staff member regarding a reprimand, union (association) issue, or evaluation topic, document the conversation.

As the assistant principal, you will encounter dozens of issues daily. Documentation is critical for two reasons: (1) it serves as a record for your memory if an issue believed to be settled is brought into question; (2) it serves as a reminder of things you have asked others to do and statements you have made, and eliminates the tag of forgetful or absent minded when others judge your job performance. Documentation will be an important function if a decision made by the assistant principal is ever brought into the court system, or less formally, if someone were to make suggestions or accusations later regarding statements made during a closed door meeting.

In addition, many teachers are now discovering documentation to be an integral function in their job descriptions as well. Consider the model presented by Charlotte Danielson (used widely as a model for effective teaching and observation); it includes in its fourth domain entitled, "Professional Responsibilities," a section on record keeping and communication (Danielson, 1996). All school personnel have occasion to dialogue with the community, but as the assistant principal in the building you will have the greatest opportunity to serve as the individual needing parent support. Just as a teacher needs to converse with the family for successful teaching, you must communicate with the public if you are going to succeed in your responsibilities as an assistant principal.

Documentation falls under two ISLLC standards: the routine management skills required for the day-to-day operations of the building (standard 3) and the legal standard should the need to defend one's actions arise in the future (standard 6). Further, one should examine the state and local laws regarding administrative notes and the issue of what is considered to be public record.

As a means of reflection and potential dialogue with a mentor, consider the following scenario and discussions.

DOCUMENTATION SCENARIO

During the third week of the school year, John Smith, a parent of a student, called and asked the assistant principal the following question, "If my son, Nicholas, misses school this Friday to take a long weekend with the family, will that hurt him academically later in the year?" The assistant principal informed the parent that missing school for vacation purposes is never a good idea when they have the summer and other vacation opportunities built into the school calendar. Nevertheless, school policy allowed for students to have three

or fewer excused vacation days per year and Nicholas was only missing one. The assistant principal asked that Nicholas inform his teachers of the absence ahead of time, acquire all the work he would be
missing, and make certain to provide all work upon his return to
school. The assistant principal hung up the telephone, jotted a few
notes from the conversation, and proceeded with his day.

Months passed and the conversation was well forgotten. In the
last month of the school year, students with exemplary attendance
were permitted to exempt all or part of their final exams, provided
they had perfect attendance and earned a letter grade of "A" on
each quarter's report card. Obviously, Nicholas was ineligible for
the attendance portion of the incentive and was distraught when
he discovered that he had worked extremely hard to qualify academically for the exemption in his most difficult course. As a result, he would be required to take the final examination.

The next day, Mr. Smith called to complain. He called the principal of the high school and informed him what his assistant had
stated months ago, that Nicholas was allowed to go with the family
and this would not hurt him academically in any way later in the
year. Mr. Smith stated that he was frustrated that the assistant principal would go back on his word and now his son was being punished after months of hard work and diligence. "After all," Mr.
Smith stated, "we are talking about a student who has never been
in trouble, has only missed one day of school, is well-liked by his
peers, and represents the school well." The principal informed Mr.
Smith that he would look into the matter and would be contacting
him at his earliest convenience.

Discussion Questions for
the Assistant Principal and Mentor

1. Which ISLLC standard best relates to this situation? (Remember, many situations relate to more than one standard.)
2. How would proper note-taking skills aid the assistant principal in the preceding scenario?

If the administration were to give in and allow Nicholas to partake in the exemption incentives, how would that decision affect the culture/tone of the school? (Which ISLLC standard addresses this particular issue with the scenario?)

A. Another way to improve documentation skills is to place yourself in hypothetical scenarios. Interview an administrative colleague to determine the legal issues regarding notes and documentation. Determine if there is local board policy regarding this issue. If the administrative notes are kept separate from a student's permanent record, does this alter the manner in which the court system views administrative notes?

B. Using the form provided at the end of this chapter, document two conversations with a student, colleague, mentor, or superior (see figure 4.1). Create a file or folder for docu-

---

Date _____   Time _____

Phone/Conversation with: _____

Regarding (Issue): _____

Summary of Conversation:

_____

_____

_____

_____

_____

_____

_____

Figure 4.1.   Sample Documentation Form

mentation to be held in the event that a review of the conversation is necessary.

C. Role Play: Assume the role of the assistant principal and ask your mentor, principal, or educational colleague to assume the role of the parent frustrated by the incentive decision. Conduct a dialogue and attempt to reach an understanding regarding the situation discussed in the documentation scenario.

D. Begin to review the additional discussion scenarios presented in chapter 12 of the text.

5

DISCIPLINE ISSUES

Often the assistant principal is the police officer of the building, regardless of the building level in education. In the elementary, the middle, or the high school, the assistant principal will fulfill the role as the first line in dealing with discipline and student misconduct issues. As an administrator, you will make literally dozens of decisions daily on a multitude of issues. Each decision will provide an opportunity for criticism—and as a first-year administrator, you will be under a microscope. Everyone wants to see how the rookie handles the precarious situations. Be prepared for this experience.

There will be classroom teachers who will rehash the discipline issues in the lunchroom and attempt to second-guess the decisions made by the administrative team. Unfortunately, these situations will arise, and all assistant principals must be prepared to face being a topic of conversation in the teacher workroom. Further, it can be very frustrating when staff members question the administrator's decisions, with minimal facts, and the administrator does not have the ability to control the grapevine or is often the last to know when decisions are second-guessed. If an individual does not have the personality to accept this form of second-guessing, administration will be one of the least fulfilling and most frustrating experiences in his/her career.

Incidentally, with some insight, many administrators can be quite adept at using the grapevine to control this discussion. Some leaders may choose to discuss some of the true facts regarding volatile, hot topic issues with the "movers and shakers" on the staff. However, keep in mind this method to control rumors could be problematic as well, for all administrators should be leery of divulging private, student discipline information to staff members. Overall, do your best to control and respond to the grapevine criticism, but do not allow it to determine your decisions.

Preparation can make the responsibility much easier. Before school begins, the entry-year administrator *must* take the opportunity to review the student handbook (ISLLC standard 3). This is the guiding factor for the discipline in the school setting. If you, as the entry-year administrator, or the assistant principal fail in this responsibility, you are choosing to discredit the work of those who have held the position previously and may be destined to repeat the mistakes of the past. Further, many assistant principals have created problems for themselves by enforcing rules that do not exist, choosing to follow their own philosophy rather than that of the community and the policies adopted by the board of education.

Understanding it is impossible to completely take one's philosophy and individual interpretation out of the equation when dealing with and enforcing school policy, it is vital you understand your role in the community at large. Every community has its own norms and history. What may be taboo in one community may be totally acceptable in another. It is your responsibility to understand how your views fit and correlate with the community at large if you are to be successful (ISLLC standard 1). If an issue appears to be taking on a life of its own, you would be wise to solicit advice from a trusted colleague who has been in the community for an extended period of time.

Further, discipline is one of the greatest issues cited by discontented parents who believe their son or daughter was treated unfairly or discriminated against because of any number of factors, such as race, their position in the community, economic status, or dealings with past administrators (ISLLC standard 5). As stated previously, many issues or tasks can apply to more than one standard and the discipline of students is just one example in this illustration.

Read the following scenario and be prepared to answer the questions that follow.

DISCIPLINE SCENARIO I

As a fundraiser, the athletic boosters have an annual "Monte Carlo Night," which involves gambling with casino-like activities. The new assistant principal is personally against the idea of gambling to raise funds and feels it is not a good example for the youth of the community and the students attending the school. Some staff members have expressed concern over this practice before, but it is quite lucrative and has greatly enhanced the athletic opportunities for the district. The student handbook expressly prohibits gambling by the students and cites a three-day out-of-school suspension for violators. A small group of students has approached the assistant principal asking, "If we cannot do this, why is it permissible for the adults to do so?"

The annual event is held in the school gymnasium and is widely attended. In fact, more community people attend Monte Carlo Night than virtually any function held at the school each year. Students attend the function and assist in the fundraising activities (though not by dealing cards or filling adult positions).

Shortly after the evening, some students are caught in their study hall engaging in the same gambling activities hosted just days before. The teacher, Ms. Jones, is outraged that students would be gambling on school grounds and brings the students to the office stating, "The past administration would not have allowed such activities and these students should be suspended immediately!"

Discussion Questions for the Assistant Principal and Mentor

1. Which ISLLC standards could be addressed by the preceding scenario?
2. How does the assistant principal's views on gambling affect how he/she should handle the misbehavior of the students?
3. How should the assistant principal address Ms. Jones's comments, if at all?
4. What is the appropriate way to address the concerns of the staff members or group of students who spoke out regarding this issue?
5. Are there legal issues that should be addressed? What are the laws regarding games of chance for fundraising in schools in your county, state, or municipality?
6. At what point should the principal be informed of the events and the discipline that is to follow?

Assistant Principal Task for Further Study

A. Assume the role of the assistant principal and ask your mentor, principal, or educational colleague to assume the role of the parent frustrated by the double standard. Conduct a dialogue and attempt to reach an understanding regarding the situation discussed in scenario #1.

This illustration is just one example of the importance of understanding your community's beliefs on certain issues. If you are new to a district or town, it would be wise to become actively involved in community groups and organizations to familiarize yourself with the norms and expectations of school personnel (ISLLC standard 6).

There may be other instances where the administrator's frustration is not with a policy or event, but rather with a staff member. Unfortunately, there are faculty members who will "bait" a child into an angry outburst, then send the student to the office for doing exactly what he/she was led to do. These moments can be most trying, as these particular staff members will usually be the first in line to criticize the administration for being unsupportive when the discipline handed down is not to their satisfaction.

Again, consider the following scenario and be prepared to answer the questions that follow.

DISCIPLINE SCENARIO 2

Mr. Hill is a science teacher in a high school in which an entry-year assistant principal has just been hired. During the course of the day, the assistant principal looks up to see a student standing in front of his/her desk. When the student is questioned, he states that Mr. Hill sent him to the office for swearing in class.

The assistant principal begins to question the student for more facts, and the student provides the following account of the day's events. The student states that he was sitting in class with his head down because in his words, "The class is so boring I can hardly stay awake." He says, "All we do day after day is listen to him talk. I cannot pay attention because we never do *anything* in that class!" Apparently, Mr. Hill stopped lecturing and told the student to pick his head up and pay attention. The student stated he followed directions, but later was caught with his head down again. The student recalled that Mr. Hill addressed him again saying, "I told you once to pay attention. It is no wonder you never pass any classes if all you do is sleep at school!"

At this point, the student stated he was frustrated but says he controlled his anger, picked up his head, and followed the directions of the teacher. Shortly after this, the student dropped his pencil and bent over to pick it up. Mr. Hill saw that he was not pay-ing attention once again and sent him to the hall. As the student was leaving, he indicated Mr. Hill told the class to "Get a good look, as this is what someone with little chance of success in life looks like." The student stated to the assistant principal that he knew it was wrong, but he was frustrated and had had enough. He told Mr. Hill, "Kiss my ass!"

The assistant principal told the student to "have a seat" because he wanted to check with Mr. Hill to make certain he had all the facts in order before addressing the situation. He approached Mr. Hill's classroom and called him to the hall for a brief discussion. The assistant principal restated the student's story as the student had told it and wanted verification from Mr. Hill. Mr. Hill agreed with the student's account of the class and indicated that he had been teaching for twenty-six years, and he was sick of these students who did not want to learn. He further indicated he "does not want that student back in his class under any circumstances!"

Discussion Questions for the Assistant Principal and Mentor

1. Which ISLLC standards are addressed by scenario 2?
2. Did Mr. Hill handle the student properly? If not, should the assistant principal address the situation or ask the principal to handle the staff member?
3. In your opinion, what should the student receive as punishment for his actions?
4. Do you believe this will be an issue later as more staff members learn about the situation through the grapevine?
5. At what point should the principal be notified of the day's events?
6. If a student came to the assistant principal later and declared, "Mr. Hill does that to students all the time," how should the assistant principal address the concerns of that student?

7. Can you think of a situation in which a teacher would be overruled in his/her punishment of a student? Please describe. Is it appropriate/permissible for the assistant principal to alter the punishment given by a staff member? Why or why not?

Assistant Principal Task for Further Study

A. Assume the role of the assistant principal and ask your mentor, principal, or educational colleague to assume the role of Mr. Hill. Pretend you are in the hallway conducting the investigation and addressing the staff member's concerns regarding student behavior.
B. Review the following additional discussion scenario with another administrator or mentor and discuss the questions provided.

DISCUSSION SCENARIO

A student entered the office and complained that a staff member was acting inappropriately. The student informed the assistant principal that during class, "Mr. Jones repeatedly yells at students, using profanity." Examples cited by the student include, "Shut the hell up!" or "Sit your ass down and be quiet!" The assistant principal asked how long this has been continuing and the student replied, "It has been happening all year, but the students are scared to do anything because they think Mr. Jones will fail them if they complain." Further, the student asked that his name not be mentioned, as he is fearful of repercussions.

- What should the assistant principal do in this situation?
- Should the principal be informed of this student's accusations?

- Should the information be included in Mr. Jones's formal evaluation?
- What should the assistant principal tell the student regarding this discussion?

It is important to note that the majority of staff members are professional and would not have handled the situation as described above. There are moments, however, when staff members make "heat of the moment" decisions that can make a small situation erupt to a much larger incident at a moment's notice. A constant tightrope to walk for every assistant principal when dealing with discipline issues is the student-teacher relationship. The situation discussed in scenario 2 illustrates the dilemma: If you agree with the student, you do not support your teachers, and if you agree with the teacher, the students will state, "It does not matter what I think or say, you will always side with the teachers. Kids are irrelevant in this school!"

Discipline issues are seldom easy and, many times, the administrator is (or should be) the unbiased person in the middle. As the first administrator in line to handle an issue, you may encounter strong emotional feelings or anger, frustration, rage, or even sadness by the participants. You must remain in control. Situations will only escalate and intensify if you lose your temper and aggravate an already angry student. This is not to say that an assistant principal should be an emotionless drone, speaking in monotone and referencing handbooks and board policy each day. It is appropriate to show emotion occasionally, as the "effect" can be successful in the right circumstances. This should be tempered; as any method of motivation, if overly used, will eventually prove unsuccessful.

As you grow in the position of dealing with discipline, you will soon discover, in most occurrences, all discipline is a matter of perception. Consider the fact that when an issue reaches the assistant principal's desk, there are immediately three distinct versions of the events which have taken place: the student's, the teacher's, and the administrator's belief after hearing both sides.

Many times, the student's perspective is based on the events that occurred on *that day*, while the teacher's perspective often is the result of frustration building that eventually led to his/her breaking point. In many instances, the student views the teacher as a professional, and this brings a certain level of "unequivocal forgiveness." The student believes that he/she should begin each day with a clean slate and all transgressions are forgiven by the ringing of the bell to end the class. The teacher, on the other hand, being quite human, is prone to memory. In many circumstances, although it is unprofessional, teachers may actually not only remember past transgressions, but also dread the student appearing in class each day.

The following discipline situation can illustrate this point.

DISCIPLINE SITUATION 3

A student was sent to the assistant principal's office. At first, the student was questioned as to what events precipitated his being sent to the office. The student replied, "I forgot my pencil and book." The assistant principal was instantly agitated at this response, as he was currently finishing a school improvement report the principal has asked him to complete on short notice. He stated to the student, "You must have done more than forget your pencil and textbook to be sent to the office. What exactly happened?" The student replied once more, "Nothing, we started class and the teacher told us to take out our homework. I had nothing with me so she sent me to the office."

Further, the student commented that he was upset because there were two individuals sitting around him who did not have their books and the teacher told them, "You will need to move closer to your neighbors so you can share their books." He also stated that another student dropped his pencil, muttered, "Damn it" and was merely told to, "Watch your mouth and sit down!" The student said he knew he should have his book, but it did not seem fair to be singled out in this manner when other students did the same thing or worse and did not require removal from class.

Again, the assistant principal was agitated at such a trivial occurrence being handled with a visit to the office, so he told the student to remain seated and he would return. He walked to the classroom and asked the teacher to step outside for a moment. As the assistant principal rehashed the student's version of events, he asked the teacher, "What exactly caused him to be sent to the office?" The teacher stated that she was at her wit's end. This particular student had not brought his book to class a total of thirteen times in the last three weeks. Further, he indicated he had lost his original book, so the teacher had assigned him a new book, and the student now stated he could not find that book either. Further, she had contacted the parents, assigned him extra work, made him sit in the hall, given him after-school detentions, and even assigned him a peer "watchdog" to remind him to bring his book and materials to class.

The assistant principal then asked if the other students were handled the way the student had reported. The teacher replied, "Yes, I told them they could share, as this was the first time they did not have materials." She also stated to the assistant principal, "I thought it would be a greater injustice to send all three to speak with you, as they should not jump right to the administrative level when he had numerous chances before this occasion to get organized." The teacher apologized for sending the student, and the assistant principal returned to the office to speak with the student.

Discussion Questions for
the Assistant Principal and Mentor

1. As stated previously, every situation creates an opportunity to evaluate the participant's perspective. Briefly, describe the

perspective of the student, the teacher and the assistant principal.

2. In your opinion, was the teacher justified in sending the student to the office?

3. Should the assistant principal punish the student? If so, what punishment would you recommend?

4. How do you think the student will present the information to his parents when he returns home for the evening and informs them he was sent to the office by his teacher? What do you predict will be his parents' reaction?

5. If the teacher came to the office after school to discuss the situation, what are some things the assistant principal should mention, should the teacher need to deal with this student in the future?

In summary, as you begin to deal with discipline issues as an administrator, you will soon recognize the complexities of the situations that arise. You must examine not only the policies and rules that govern the students, but also the social norms, past practices, and most important, the needs of the student in determining your decisions regarding student discipline.

6

SPECIAL EDUCATION ISSUES

Having already discussed some of the issues with discipline, it is important to take the opportunity to evaluate the entry-year assistant principal's knowledge of the Individuals with Disabilities Education Act (IDEA) and how it pertains to the role of the assistant principal. As the assistant principal, you may be asked to be the administrative representative during a student's annual Individualized Education Program (IEP) meeting. You may also encounter discipline situations with special education students. Your success as an administrator will be closely tied to your understanding of the legal aspects surrounding the discipline of special needs students.

The administrative resources for special education services vary greatly from district to district, thus leaving the expertise of the administration in this area to vary greatly as well. For our purposes, I will attempt to mention the most pertinent aspects of this legislation and attempt to provide a glimpse of the legal aspects of special education students (ISLLC standards 3 and 6).

An enormous amount of time can be exhausted working with special education students, as their needs are greater than the majority of the student population. Further, many districts have lost large sums of money in legal battles relating to special education services. If you were to survey a population of administrators and ask questions regarding special education responsibilities, you would undoubtedly hear tales of woe and dismay from their experienced colleagues. Fortunately, if entry-year administrators are trained and prepared properly, many such instances can be prevented and ultimately, the district and all students will benefit.

Engage in some professional dialogue with a colleague who is knowledgeable in special education legislation and procedures, and you will learn there are rules for dealing with special education students that must be taken into consideration before you rush to judgment. For instance, legislation has placed a limit of ten days out-of-school suspension before certain guidelines are enacted when disciplining special needs students. You may find it helpful to ascertain if your district has policies, procedures, or paperwork to complete when dealing with special education students.

Before you examine special education case studies and scenarios, it is imperative that you recognize special education terminology and understand how those terms relate to student issues. Review the following list of terms with a special education coordinator, consultant, school psychologist, or administrator, and develop a working definition before progressing further with this chapter. These terms are not meant to be all-inclusive of special education; they are merely a starting point for those individuals who are beginning administrative roles that regularly deal with special education students, faculty, and families (ISLLC standards 2, 3, and 6).

The following definitions were obtained from *Learning Disabilities: Theories, Diagnosis, and Teaching Strategies* by Janet Lerner (2000), *Model Policies and Procedures for the Education of Children with Disabilities* by the Ohio Department of Education (2000), and the following websites: www.parentpals.com and www.specialeducationlawyers.info.

Attention Deficit Disorder (ADD) or Attention Deficit Hyperactivity Disorder (ADHD)—Students with this condition are characterized with difficulty staying on task and concentrating. It may or may not be accompanied by hyperactivity.

Bipolar Disorder—This diagnosis is characterized as a major affective disorder in which an individual alternates between states of deep depression and extreme elation.

Functional Behavioral Assessment—This first serves as an assessment to better understand a child's behavior, then systematically determines the driving forces behind that behavior.

Individualized Education Program (IEP)—The written plan for the education of an individual student with learning disabilities. The plan must meet the requirements specified in the rules and regulations of IDEA.

Individuals with Disabilities Education Act (IDEA)—The special education law ensuring that students with disabilities have a free, appropriate public education (FAPE).

Intervention Assessment Team (IAT)—Often the precursor to special education programs, it serves as a meeting for a group of educators to develop strategies to work with individual students. Subsequent meetings reflect on student progress in response to developed interventions.

Manifestation Hearing—When dealing with the discipline of a special education student, it may be necessary to determine if the child's behavior was a direct result of his/her disability. The manifestation hearing should be held before any change of placement is completed.

Multi-Factored Evaluation (MFE)—The evaluation piece for the identification of students for special education programs.

Special Education Child Advocate—Someone representing the interests of children with disabilities, frequently an attorney.

Special Education Categories (may change frequently)

> *Cognitively Disabled (CD)*—often referred to "Developmentally Handicapped," children in this category have lower IQ scores with mildly *mentally retarded* characteristics.
>
> *Specific Learning Disability (SLD)*—A severe learning problem due to a disorder in the basic psychological processes involved in acquiring, organizing, or expressing information.
>
> *Multiple Disabilities (MD)*—People with severe disabilities are those who traditionally have been labeled as having severe to profound mental retardation. These people require ongoing, extensive support in more than one major life activity in order to participate in integrated community settings and enjoy the quality of life available to people with fewer or no disabilities. They frequently have additional disabilities, including movement difficulties, sensory losses, and behavior problems.
>
> *Emotionally Disturbed (ED)*—Characterized clinically by lacking the feeling of trust, respect, and family love. If severe, the disturbance is at a greater level with proven diagnosis in one or more of the following:
>
> - schizophrenia
> - bipolar disorder
> - major depression
> - obsessive compulsive disorder
> - panic disorder
> - eating disorder
> - autism
> - serious emotional disturbance in children and adolescents
>
> *Severely Behaviorally Handicapped (SBH)*—Disability characteristic in which students are emotionally disturbed or socially maladjusted.

Traumatic Brain Injury (TBI)—A student who before, during, or after birth has received an injury to or suffered an infection of the brain. As a result of such impairment, there are disturbances that prevent or impede the normal learning processes.

Other Health Impairment (OHI)—Having an extenuating disability classified under IDEA.

Read the following special education scenarios and be prepared to answer the questions that follow.

SPECIAL EDUCATION SCENARIO I

During lunch one afternoon, the supervisor in the cafeteria brought two students into the office to see the assistant principal. One of the boys was bleeding from his nose, and the other had a small cut above his right eye. It was quickly evident that the students had been in a skirmish of some kind. The teacher indicated he noticed, out of the corner of his eye, a commotion brewing and began to make his way toward the noises. By the time the teacher had arrived, there was a group of students yelling, and these two students were wrestling around on the floor.

Apparently, the two students, Timothy and James, were arguing over a rumor that Timothy had approached James's girlfriend about going to the movies that afternoon. James took offense to this intrusion and decided to approach Timothy in the lunchroom. What began as a question and show of courage quickly escalated and became violent. Further, James was a student who had been in the office frequently and had been warned about his excessive number of discipline referrals. Timothy, too, had been in the office on numerous occasions. The assistant principal had attempted to work with Timothy, as he was a special needs student with an SLD and he required much attention. Further, Timothy had currently been suspended for a total of *eight* days for two incidents involving tobacco at school and a previous altercation with another student.

Put yourself in the position of assistant principal and determine your next course of action. The questions below should serve as a guide in determining your options.

1. Determine how the following terms researched above relate to the special education scenario above.
   IDEA
   SLD
   multi-factored evaluation
   functional behavioral assessment
   manifestation hearing
2. Which ISLLC standards apply to the special education scenario and the legal issues that could ensue?
3. Is there justification to punish both students? If so, should they be punished equally? What does your current school district handbook state as policy for addressing student violence/fighting?
4. Based on the preliminary administrative meeting conducted as part of the chapter 1 exercises, would this be an issue to involve the principal? Why or why not?
5. Would this situation change if Timothy had an SBH classification? If so, how?

The first scenario is precisely the type of event for which every assistant principal should be prepared—regardless of level (elementary, middle, or high school). The discipline of special needs students never appears to be black-and-white. There always appears to be more to consider than just dealing with the behavior. Some students or situations can be much more severe. Consider the second example with the discipline of a special needs student.

SPECIAL EDUCATION SCENARIO 2

As the assistant principal was making her morning rounds, one of the educational aides came rushing up and exclaimed, "We are having problems with her again!" The assistant principal knew right away about whom the aide was speaking. One of the students in the multi-handicapped classroom, Melissa, had a reputation for being *extremely* disruptive. As the assistant principal rushed to the classroom and peered into the window in the door, she could see the situation. Melissa was running about in the classroom and she had taken every clothing item off, with the exception of her red, high-top sneakers. There were no other students in the room, but Melissa was literally destroying the classroom. She had defecated in one of the corners of the room and was throwing the feces about the room. This student was an absolute mess and now, so was the classroom.

Unfortunately, this was not the first such incident for Melissa. She was a student with multiple disabilities, including Down's syndrome. She was classified as MD and SBH. During her IEP meeting, the school district had argued that the local school was probably not the best placement for her. Melissa's parents insisted, and as financial concerns are always a consideration when placing special education students, Melissa was placed in the district multi-handicapped classroom.

Melissa was not the only student in the class. There were five other students, each with severe disabilities. One student required a nurse at all times, had no movement from the neck down, and was on a breathing apparatus. Other students also were diagnosed with Down's syndrome, but did not have the SBH classification. The highest-functioning student in the room was an autistic student who needed much less assistance. For the five students in the classroom one full-time teacher, one nurse, and two aides were assigned.

The assistant principal asked how Melissa had gotten time to engage in these activities and the aide explained the other students had gone to gym class. Melissa had stayed behind to change in the room, as she could not be around the other students when changing, due to her continued disruptive behavior. During the course of the change, she began to have the accident in her pants. As the aide turned to get some cleaning supplies, Melissa had broken away and the melee began.

Melissa had been punished before, and the assistant principal was frustrated at the number of occurrences when Melissa had injured others in the classroom and she had to field the phone calls from concerned/angry parents. Unfortunately, she was at a loss and was uncertain as to how to handle the situation.

Discussion Questions for the
Assistant Principal and Mentor

1. Which of the special education vocabulary terms apply to this scenario?
2. What do you perceive is the assistant principal's first course of action? Second? Third?
3. Describe the moral/ethical implications of this scenario for Melissa, the other students in the classroom, the teacher and the aides, and the administration.
4. What role do the finances of the district serve in the scenario presented above?
5. What punishment do you believe is warranted in this situation?

Not all special education situations are as serious as the one described above, and not all special education issues are discipline related. The category of "special education" is varied and the students differ in many respects; therefore, it is often difficult to distinguish between those students who cannot possibly understand their actions, those students who need assistance, and those students who truly take advantage of the system they have been provided.

As an administrator, you will hear all sides to the special education debate. This may involve funds allocated for special education, accommodations the students receive in the classroom, or the perceived extra duties teachers may encounter when a student with special needs is placed in their class. This will be an important issue, and you will need more than a basic knowledge of special education law, policies, and guidelines if you are going to be successful in the administrative arena.

7

ATTENDANCE ISSUES

Virtually every administrator with whom I have spoken has listed student attendance as one aspect of his/her job description. Every handbook in every school will list attendance rules and regulations. In reviewing this chapter, it will be extremely helpful to have a copy of the attendance rules and regulations for the school district in which you are employed.

Past practice is also an important aspect to be researched when addressing school attendance. Many districts have laws on the books that are rarely enforced. For instance, in some districts it may be entirely permissible to miss school for the first day of hunting season or to show livestock at the local county fair. Realizing that most districts or states do not *officially* recognize these events in their legislation, it is important to understand the larger social norms of the community in which you work (ISLLC standards 1, 3, and 6)

To illustrate this point, the first activity assigned for this chapter is a comparison of school attendance policies. Research your student handbook and/or board of education policy regarding the following attendance issues. Then, after you have reviewed the guidelines for your district, engage in a dialogue with a colleague serving a similar role in another district and compare/contrast the same issues with his/her student handbook. The following chart should assist you with this project (see figure 7.1).

As you progress in your experiences, you will discover that attendance could make you *the most deceived person in the district*. Parents many times have the perception, "The school forces us to lie." Read the following attendance scenario and be prepared to complete the activity that follows.

District:
          (A)   **(B)**

_____   _____

Vacation days—Are they allowed? How many are acceptable?

_____   _____

_____   _____

_____   _____

Truancy—What is the district's definition of truancy? What are the consequences?

_____   _____

_____   _____

_____   _____

Number of Allowable *Excused* Absences—

_____   _____

_____   _____

_____   _____

What constitutes a "Half-Day" absence vs. a student who is "Tardy" or just late?

_____   _____

_____   _____

_____   _____

Figure 7.1.   Attendance Chart

If a student is involved in athletics, what percentage of the day must he/she be present to participate that evening? Is there a clause for weekend events if a student is absent on the Friday before the weekend?

_____   _____

_____   _____

_____   _____

_____   _____

_____   _____

_____   _____

_____

Are there incentives available for students with exemplary attendance? Are there exceptions to this rule (i.e., physician's note, funeral of family member, etc.) which allow a student to still receive the incentives?

_____   _____

_____   _____

_____

Will students receive academic repercussions for excessive absences from school? If so, what is the number before these consequences take place? Is this based on quarterly, semester, or yearly time frames?

_____   _____

_____   _____

_____   _____

What attendance resources are available to the assistant principal (i.e., resource officer, court systems liaison, specialist, etc…)?

_____   _____

_____   _____

_____   _____

What is the step-by-step procedure for students with excessive absences?

Step #1

_____   _____

_____   _____

(continued)

Step #2

_____   _____

_____   _____

Step #3

_____   _____

_____   _____

Step #4

_____   _____

_____   _____

What is the procedure for students who leave school early due to illness? How are the teachers notified?

_____   _____

_____   _____

_____   _____

What is the penalty for an *Unexcused* **Absence?**

_____   _____

_____   _____

_____   _____

List any further differences between the districts identified with your comparison.

Figure 7.1. (*continued*)

ATTENDANCE SCENARIO 1

Johnny was tired because he did not get back from the basketball game until 11:00 P.M. and he did not have an opportunity to finish his homework. In support of their son, the parents called Johnny in sick and informed the secretary he would be arriving around 10:00 A.M. "after he had a chance to wake up, get some breakfast, and get moving." Privately, these parents argued, "If I had called in and said he needed to sleep due to the game, this would have been an unexcused absence and that would hurt him academically." In most circumstances, his parents would be correct. The assistant principal was frustrated as Johnny had been "sick" for a couple of hours in the morning, coincidentally, after every night game, as his teammates managed to make it on time.

In this situation, parents need to understand the attendance rules are in place to teach good, lifelong, employability habits. Any organization will contend employee absenteeism is a concern. Further, parents must also be made to understand it is extremely difficult to teach Johnny if he is not present, and this situation is unfair to his morning teachers and his teammates who happen to make it on time. Lastly, it is unfair to teach Johnny by enabling him to justify false statements as long as it benefits him in some way.

Fairness is always an issue with attendance (ISLLC standard 5). Some parents will need to be reassured when they are honest and forthright with the school/administration, causing their son/daughter to miss out on some school incentive. At the same time, these same parents may see a neighbor be dishonest as their child faces no repercussions.

Further, the issue above relates to high school *and* athletic policies. It is important for the assistant principal or the administrator in charge of attendance to understand the overlap between attendance rules and other sectors of the school community.

Of course, some students do have legitimate medical reasons for chronic absenteeism, and most attendance guidelines have loopholes to deal with such occurrences. For instance, most rational administrators would not attempt to academically fail a student on the basis of absenteeism after the student was diagnosed with leukemia and was missing school for chemotherapy treatments and other related medical treatments. The assistant principal must be prepared to address those students who wish to take advantage of loopholes designed to assist truly needy students.

Discussion Questions for the
Assistant Principal and Mentor

1. Assume the position of the assistant principal and engage in a conversation with Johnny's mother or father. Be prepared to utilize the attendance rules applicable in your district's student code of conduct. Complete the sample documentation form in chapter 4 and record the main points of the conversation.

ATTENDANCE SCENARIO 2

A teacher entered the assistant principal's office soon after the beginning of the school day. He had a student in his morning class who was acting strangely and appeared to be "out of it." The teacher felt this particular student was under the influence of some type of drug or alcohol. The teacher expressed the student was unusually talkative, slurred his speech at times, and seemed to have trouble keeping his eyes wide open.

Discussion Questions for the
Assistant Principal and Mentor

1. What do you do with the teacher's information?
2. What could the repercussions be if the student was wrongly accused of substance abuse?
3. What advice would you give other teachers who suspect this type of behavior?

After reviewing the scenarios and tasks associated with this chapter, you should recognize the importance of both reviewing policy and expecting the unique trials associated with school attendance issues. You will almost certainly be deceived and tested when addressing some students and their parents/guardians. Often, it is important to examine the student's history to determine if there is an underlying reason for his/her failure to willingly attend school. Proper documentation, investigation, and research are often necessary to handle attendance issues successfully.

8

LEAVING THE ONE-ROOM SCHOOL HOUSE

As you leave the classroom and enter the world of administration, you will be amazed at the different ability levels and teaching styles of those who now report to you. As a classroom teacher, I had the opportunity to eat with fellow teachers, attend staff meetings, or even socialize after school with these same individuals. Having gotten to know my colleagues on a personal level, I felt I knew them on a professional level as well. Nothing could have been further from the truth!

Unfortunately, most teachers today still, as in the early days of education, teach their classes in isolation and seldom watch others perform in their craft. As an entry-year administrator, you will have the opportunity to conduct a walk-through of the building as part of your daily routine. You will gain valuable insight into the teacher's role as you follow students throughout the course of the day. This will provide the assistant principal the opportunity to reflect on the proper supervision of teachers and to witness the actions that separate one teacher from another. Many administrators have made the comment, "I would be a much better teacher now if I ever go back into the classroom." Probably the biggest reason for this statement is the administrator's ability to see the larger picture and the events that take place in *every* classroom in the building.

Critical to the success of any administrator is leaving the office and being visible in the hallways, classrooms, and lunchroom. It is extremely easy to become entrenched in the piles of work and discipline referrals in the office and stay hidden from the student population. Further, the assistant principal enjoys the best opportunity to make personal connections with students in social settings outside the office. For instance, some of the best interactions I enjoyed were during the hours of cafeteria supervision. Lunch provided an opportunity to meet with students on nonofficial business. Consider the following example:

> In most school systems, it is a rite of passage for the teachers to move to the front of the lunch line. A good public relations technique is to purchase the lunch for the student who allows you to step in front of him/her to receive your lunch. As finances are tight with all educators, I must admit I did not use this tactic every day. However, I did regularly attempt to use this strategy with students whom I had just recently disciplined in some way. It was my way of stating, "I did not like what you did and I had to do my job, but it does not mean that I believe you should be removed from the school and discarded." The look on most students' faces after the assistant principal just gave them a discipline referral and then proceeded to buy him/her lunch an hour later was priceless and well worth the minimal expense of a school lunch. (This is an example of ISLLC standard 5.)

Another suggestion for positive student interaction is during the time when report cards are sent to the students. Each quarter, students will receive some type of progress or grade card. In every year of my administrative tenure, I have used this time as an opportunity for positive student/community relations. Before grade cards were issued, the principal and I would divide the school in half and *personally sign* each student's report card. If the grades were unacceptable, we took the time to write a short note stating this fact and requesting a conference with "see me" written across the bottom of the report card.

This strategy allowed us to complete two vital aspects of student administration interaction. In addition to emphasizing our concern for academic success, this was another attempt to meet with students for academic, rather than discipline purposes. For more successful follow-through, I would suggest you maintain a list of the students who were given such a command, as many may fail to appear for the meeting. In addition, if a student's grades were exceptional, we would also take the time to comment on their accomplishments.

Students and parents love to see the extra recognition. Many administrators would state, "My school is too big and I cannot possibly take the time for this." If you are the assistant principal in a large building, encourage your principal and guidance counselors to assist with this process. If you lack the authority to require such assistance and your principal does not see the benefits of such a strategy, take the opportunity to sign and meet with those students who seem to find their way to the office on a regular basis for discipline referrals. Regardless of the assistance you may receive, this process is strongly suggested. I have personally signed or witnessed the signing of nearly five hundred report cards in an evening. It is my belief that the administration has time to accomplish the tasks they designate as a priority; I encourage making academic student connections a priority.

The individual meetings are also worth the required extra time. Having a meeting about their academic standing with an administrator may be new for most students, and this will provide an opportunity for the administrator to establish some rapport. A frequent complaint from the parents of student dropouts may be, "My son/daughter was failing and nobody at that school cared." These meetings will pay large dividends in reducing these types of statements. Further, the next time the administration must meet with the parents on a discipline issue (and he/she undoubtedly will), the assistant principal has sent the message that he/she cares for that student and his/her academic success. The school will cease to have the image of being a callous organization that merely processes students and views everyone as a number on a roll (IS-LLC standard 5).

The previous methods of gaining respect and rapport with students are merely examples of reaching out to students and community. Take a moment to review the following questions and activities with your mentor regarding student/administrator interactions.

1. How important is the student/administrator relationship to the effectiveness of the first-year administrator?
2. How much time should the assistant principal spend *out* of the office on a daily basis for activities such as hall monitoring, classroom visitations, meetings, etc.?
3. What should the ratio of negative student interaction (discipline) to positive student interaction (praise, academic assistance, casual conversation, etc.) be for the assistant principal?

Tasks for the assistant principal to increase understanding:

Activity 1—Engage in discussions with (at least) *three* experienced administrators and their methods for student interaction. Compare those with the examples given and determine the *one* method that you would like to attempt this year.

Activity 2—During the course of the next year, conduct as least *five* meetings with students regarding academic progress. Using the documentation discussed in chapter 3, document the need for the meeting, the issues discussed, the interventions discussed to assist the student, and the effectiveness of those interventions.

Activity 3—Track your duties for one week, noting the time spent on each activity. Calculate the percentage of time spent with both positive and negative student interaction. Compare those percentages with the answer you gave in question 3 above. Was your answer similar to your *actual* activities conducted?

Activity 4—Review *one* additional discussion scenario presented in chapter 9 of the text.

Just as teachers should be encouraged to share ideas and engage in professional dialogue, administrators should take the lead and serve as a role model for these activities. The faculty and staff of your building should not close the door to their classrooms and teach in their one-room school house; likewise, the administrator should not be trapped day after day in the office and fail to see the benefits of personal interaction with students and staff. It has been said many times, education is a people business and the skills needed to work with people will be the most important attributes for any first-year administrator.

COURT RULINGS AND THEIR IMPACT ON ADMINISTRATIVE DECISIONS

Undoubtedly, the assistant principal will have the unfortunate opportunity to make a decision that *could* ultimately end up in the legal system. Any discipline situation that takes a student out of the classroom setting could potentially wind up as a civil rights issue. ISLLC standard 6 addresses the need for the entry-year administrator to understand the larger social, economic, and legal issues surrounding the educational process. Since the assistant principal is usually the first administrator to address student issues, you will be the first in the series of due process procedures.

As a result of your initial involvement in this process, it is imperative you understand not only the board policies of the district, but also the rulings and interpretations of the judicial system involving educational matters. You must also realize the courts continually revisit issues, and decisions are frequently overturned or reversed. While this makes it difficult for any school administrator to become an expert in the field of school law, all school officials must be at least adequately prepared to address the ever-changing landscape of school discipline and student rights.

Following are several cases that have changed the perception of school discipline, dress codes, and various other policies involving the school setting. Again, as with many other sections of this manual, the issues stressed with the following court cases involve the issues historically related to the assistant principal position. This is not to claim the legal cases described are the most important to the educational setting today, but they are directly related to the concerns and responsibilities of the typical assistant principal position. As with the ISLLC standards it is not important to be expected to memorize cases and decisions by the court system, but it is important to understand the present tone the courts set by the decisions made.

CASE I—*TINKER V. DES MOINES INDEPENDENT COMMUNITY SCHOOL DISTRICT*

This case has been argued time and again and is often the basis for many freedom of expression claims by students and their families. In this case, three students from Des Moines, Iowa, chose to wear black armbands protesting the Vietnam War. The school had heard of this and banned this practice and warned all students if they chose to violate this policy, they would be suspended from school. The students violated the policy and were subsequently suspended. Their parents filed suit and in December 1969 the Supreme Court issued its ruling. It held that the First Amendment applied to public schools and students . . . did not shed their constitutional rights . . . at the schoolhouse gate (Rutherford Institute, n.d., p. 1). Other cases followed but the standard established by the *Tinker* case has changed slightly.

According to the Rutherford Institute, two essential criteria should be addressed when establishing school policy limiting speech or dress in the school setting: (1) the student's speech or dress must substantially interfere with the operation of the school, and (2) the student's speech must interfere with the rights of others.

This case on the surface seemed to take control over some issues away from the school and put more power in the hands of the students. Two other cases later would sway the pendulum back somewhat and give more power back to the schools. Those cases did not involve dress codes, but did affect student rights. In the cases of *Bethel v. Fraser* and *Hazelwood v. Kuhlmeier*, the courts ruled the schools did indeed have the right to control free speech for "legitimate educational purposes" (*Tinker v. Des Moines Independent School District*, 2006, p. 2).

These three cases together have come to be known as the "*Tinker* trilogy" and are used as the precedents for deciding free speech issues in regard to education. It is wise to have a basic knowledge of their history and how they are utilized when implementing policy in today's educational climate.

CASE 2—NIXON V. NORTHERN LOCAL SCHOOL DISTRICT BOARD OF EDUCATION, 383 F. SUPP. 2D 965

This is a recent case (2005) involving a U.S. District Court in southern Ohio. According to the courts, the student's First and Fourteenth Amendment rights were challenged after the district forced a student to leave school for violating school dress code policy. He had arrived to school wearing a T-shirt critical of the Islamic religion, abortion, and homosexuality. The student was also told he would be punished if he chose to wear the shirt again in the future. As with many school districts, the student handbook "prohibited students from wearing clothing considered offensive or obscene because such clothing disrupted the educational process" (Schoenfeld Crotty, 2006, p.17). In this particular case, the courts ruled the clothing did not have an "overly distracting" impact on the educational process and therefore, should not have been targeted. Further, the courts cited the *Tinker* trilogy cases as the basis for its decision.

This is one example of the need to understand how the legal system affects student code of conduct, dress codes, and discipline issues. Often entry-year administrators feel as though cases are black-and-white and easy to solve if there is a rule or policy preventing such behavior. The prepared administrator realizes most issues are never easy, and the potential for larger issues are ever present.

CASE 3—*BLAU V. FORT THOMAS PUBLIC SCHOOL DISTRICT*, 401 F.3D 381 (6TH CIR. 2005)

In this case, a parent alleged the adoption of a school dress code prohibited his daughter from expressing her individuality and thus was violating her First and Fourteenth Amendment rights. His goal was to eliminate all policies governing school dress. The court ruled in favor of the school district, stating the First Amendment does not protect such obscure definitions of freedom of speech and expression. Also, the court concluded a dress code does not constitute any particular viewpoint; instead, a dress code merely defines what clothing is permissible in the school environment. While the court agreed parents have the right to control their child's education, parents do not have the right "to bar a school from adopting a reasonable dress code" (Donovsky, 2005).

This case appears to have contradicted the *Nixon* case above and was cited to illustrate that point. Often, the courts rule in such a manner, which may lead to confusion by the administrative personnel of the school district. In the *Nixon* case discussed above, the courts clearly ruled in a manner limiting the power of the district regarding dress code issues. Conversely, the *Blau* case establishes that districts do have the ability to establish a dress code to regulate the educational process. The best advice is for the entry year administrator to exercise caution when addressing school dress code issues.

It is important for administrators to remember that often the student who wishes to challenge a district rule or policy has an agenda. Further, many times the student was instructed by a parent who may have had an issue with the district. It is best to weigh the regulations with the need to protect the interests of the school and the learning of the student body. Especially in the upper grade levels, it is necessary to ask, "Will the administration enforcing a new policy/rule create more disruption to the educational process than the student wearing the questionable clothing?" Clearly, if the answer is yes, the administration may wish to revisit the need for that particular rule in the student handbook.

CASE #4—LAYSHOCK V. HERMITAGE SCHOOL DISTRICT, 2006 WL 240655

Recent advances in technology have made certain situations in the school setting very troubling for administrators, especially those administrators who are involved in the disciplinary process. Websites such as MySpace.com have become a haven for teens to post everything from a satire of school personnel to threatening and intimidating warnings involving other members of the student body. The court system is just beginning to answer the questions regarding the lines between that which is a harmless rambling of a teenager or that which may ultimately be a warning sign of a horrendous school violence rampage. Without knowing the intent of the individual, schools are becoming increasingly aware of the messages students post and the harmful effects they may have on the educational process.

A Pennsylvania district court recently upheld a school district's decision to move an honor student to an alternative center based on a MySpace web posting involving a disrespectful portrayal of his principal. While off school grounds, the student had accessed this particular website from a computer at his grandmother's home. It did not take long for news of the website to travel to all students in the building. In fact, the site became such an issue that the school was forced to shut down computer operations, including all computer courses. The boy's parents challenged the discipline on the grounds that the school violated the student's First Amendment rights. The courts ruled in favor of the district on the grounds that the boy's actions interrupted the educational process. Further, the courts ruled the school was within its rights to discipline the student's actions even though they occurred away from school premises (Schoenfeld Crotty, 2006).

It can be difficult to handle many of the issues that arise out of student use of the Internet. "Cyber bullying" is now an issue in many of the nation's schools in which students are subjected to verbal assaults, rants, or even threats by fellow classmates. One of the primary questions to be addressed is the location of the action. Most school policies address the discipline of students who posted messages to these sites on district computers, but many districts are now forced to address the implications of postings done after school hours by tech-savvy teens on home computers.

It is strongly encouraged for student handbooks to include a section dealing with the Internet and how issues can and will be addressed that find their way into the school setting. Imagine the intimidation a student would feel if he/she had to endure constant taunts based on a website posting by a fellow classmate. It is not appropriate for the district to have a hands-off approach to these matters and stand by while students are bullied by their peers, even if it originates somewhere other than school. Ultimately, ignoring the problem could result in litigation as well for the hostile environment created by these actions.

CASE 5—PORTER V. ASCENSION PARISH SCHOOL BOARD, 393 F.3D 608 (5TH CIR. 2004)

In today's educational climate, districts are facing more and more issues involving school violence and fear associated with actions by individual students. No administrator wants to be involved in the next school shooting situation; and many districts have adopted a zero tolerance policy involving any behavior associated with any action deemed threatening or intimidating toward other students or staff. As a result of these measures the courts have seen many cases involving the discipline of students for violating an anti-violence approach.

The critical question in these types is defining exactly what a true threat is to the school. In the case of *Porter v. Ascension*, the student had drawn a picture of a person armed with a missile and torch soaking the school in gasoline. The drawing also depicted an individual throwing a brick at the principal as two students with guns were standing nearby. The student had shown the pictures to friends and family. Two years after having created the drawing, the student's younger brother inadvertently took a sketchpad to school with the picture inside. A staff member viewed the picture and took it to the principal. The student who drew the picture was expelled and reassigned to an alternative center, and his brother was suspended for being in possession of the picture. The Fifth Circuit Court ruled the drawing did not constitute a true threat, as the threat was not "knowingly communicated to either the object of the threat or a third person" (Donovsky, 2005, p. 5).

As in the issue of school dress, the courts rulings can be confusing if you were to attempt to anticipate the ruling based on past issues that appear similar. This ambiguity can be further illustrated by examining other court decisions involving the discipline of a student where the child's actions constituted a true threat to the other members of the student body.

CASE 6—D.F. V. BOARD OF EDUCATION OF SYOSSET CENTRAL SCHOOL DISTRICT, 2005 WL 2219096 (E.D.N.Y. 2005).

In this case, as part of an English assignment given by his teacher, a sixth grader wrote a story involving the sexual assault and murders of several classmates. The teacher discovered the story and presented it to the administration. The board of education suspended the student for thirty days. The boy's parents subsequently filed suit claiming his First Amendment rights were violated. This particular court found that the boy was a minor and as such was not entitled to the same First Amendment protection granted to all citizens. The courts also claimed "the graphic depictions of murder and sex in the story may materially interfere with the work of the school by disturbing students and teachers" (Donovsky, 2005, p. 6).

Again, it is difficult to attempt to anticipate how a district or state court will rule, and the preceding cases illustrate the need to examine each situation on its own merit. It is easy for the beginning administrator to utilize the student handbook as the overriding force in discipline issues. This is not meant to diminish the importance of following board policy, but all administrators are hired for their ability to rationally think and *apply* those rules.

Consider the following activities as you reflect on the importance of legal decisions on the educational process.

1. Review your school dress code with the principal or mentor and address the following questions. Does the dress code present potential problems regarding First Amendment student rights? Are the dress code issues "specific in nature" or are the rules "open and rely heavily on administrative judgment?" Have there been specific dress code violations in the past that led to the rules listed in the handbook?
2. Review your district's computer usage, bullying, and harassment policies and address the following questions. Does the policy allow for punishment of student behaviors "outside" the school day and "off school premises?" Has the district had situations arise in regard to specific websites and Internet usage? Are the teachers involved in the policing of Internet us-

age in the school setting? What training has taken place for staff members regarding these types of issues?

3. Research educational court cases to discover issues affecting your state and area. Are there other types of issues that need to be addressed by your school policy manual and student handbook? What recent rulings exist that would change the way your building currently conducts day-to-day operations?

4. Discuss with your mentor/colleague how to handle the following situation. A female student arrives at school wearing clothing that is excessively revealing. Her teacher sends her to the office for administrative input. You inform the student that her top is too revealing and offer her a shirt to wear or she must go home and change. After consulting with her parents, she leaves to change and returns with her mother. Assuming the role of a male entry-year administrator, discuss how you would address her mother's charge that you were looking at her daughter in an unprofessional manner and she "did not appreciate you checking her daughter out like that!"

5. Using the most recent version of your student handbook, read the following scenario and answer the questions that follow. A teacher brings a student into the office and asks your "opinion" regarding a student's appearance. She believes the female student's blouse is cut too low and is too revealing. Apparently, the teacher had told the student the blouse was not appropriate and an argument ensued. The teacher then brought the student to the office to avoid the incident escalating further.

- Is there a dress code policy for your building?
- Did the teacher handle the situation correctly?
- Does your decision change if the teacher had brought the student to the office at the end of the day?

- Does the "physical stature/build" of the student have any bearing on your decision?

This section of the manual is not meant to scare an individual from the administrative ranks, but it is meant to further illustrate the necessity for careful consideration before many decisions are made. It is impossible to forecast court decisions, and the successful administrator does not avoid potentially "flammable" issues to avert litigation. While you should not be expected to fully understand *every* existing legal issue in the court system, you should have knowledge of the most recent decisions that could affect your district policies and procedures if you are to be successful.

PREPARING FOR THE SUCCESSFUL PARENT MEETING

As a high school administrator, I have had the opportunity to conduct virtually dozens of parent meetings. ISLLC standard 4 addresses the importance of having regular communications with family and community members for the successful administrator. The purpose of those communications can vary widely from intervention assistance team (IAT) meetings to special education meetings (IEP) or less formal conversations regarding discipline or academic issues. Regardless of the format of the meeting, the opportunity exists for either the school administrator or the parent to leave feeling frustrated and angered by the outcome if the meeting is not successfully conducted.

Obviously, the more experienced you become in conducting parent meetings, the more likely an amicable solution will be the result. This portion of the manual is meant to lessen the learning curve as it is a chance to provide some helpful suggestions for those who find themselves in the role of facilitator for a parent meeting.

It is important for the entry-year administrator to realize most parents simply want what is best for their child. With this simple premise in mind, stay focused on the task at hand, and continue with efforts to include parents in the educational process. Research has proven again and again that when parents are involved, student achievement is more likely to take place. Knowing this, as professionals, we should continue with our efforts for the benefit of our students and the reputation of the district.

Here is a list of four strategies for the entry-year administrator to keep in mind when you conduct a parent meeting.

I. MAKE CONTACT BEFORE THE MEETING

It is vital for the school to have made parent contacts before most meetings take place. Staff members should keep documentation of phone calls and notes sent home to parents for possible review during the meeting. Refer to the sample documentation form in chapter 4 when completing records of this type.

If parents are called to the school for any "crisis" issue, they are more inclined to react in a negative manner if this is the first dealing with the administrator or school personnel. It is strongly encouraged for you as the entry-year administrator to extend the olive branch before school begins and make efforts to meet the parents. Schools routinely have open houses and meetings before the school year begins. If parents do not attend, school officials should make the effort to call and complete introductions. If a situation arises later, the parents may not feel as though the school is *out to get* their child if they have already met the administrator previously. Also, if you are forced to impose discipline on a student later, this strategy may lower the level of resistance by the parents. You are encouraged to attend as many activities as possible and to utilize strategies such as this to meet the parents in your district, as the community relations benefits are numerous and will pay dividends at a future time.

Another related idea is to deal with issues *when* they occur. Too often, administrators simply hope a situation will go away or improve *without* parent communication. It is amazing the missed opportunities many educators face by not being proactive with parent relations.

Consider the following scenario: Cindy was disruptive in class today and had to be addressed. At first she was "talkative" and the disruption was minor. The teacher asked Cindy to be quiet so class could progress. Moments later, there was another outburst, and Cindy was at the center of the disruption. The teacher addressed Cindy once again, asking for proper behavior. This time, the teacher asked her to move to the front of the room. Yet again, Cindy was disruptive and the teacher was forced to place her in the hall until she could speak with her privately.

Later the teacher went into the hall and spoke with Cindy. She told her that her behavior was unacceptable and she would be forced to serve a detention. Further, she told Cindy the behavior must stop or she would be sent to the principal's office.

After such an altercation, the staff member has a choice. Should he/she call and inform the parents of the day's events? Or should the teacher hope the situation has been addressed and proceed as though all is going to be okay in the future? For a moment, consider the consequences of each alternative action *from the parent's perspective*.

In the first method, Cindy's parents were called and informed of the day's events. The teacher rehashed the step-by-step actions she took with Cindy as the class progressed. As Cindy walked in the door, she was greeted by parents previously made well aware of her actions, and they began to question her regarding the issue. The parents had met her teacher ahead of time, and a solid rapport had been established. The teacher stated to the parents, "I did not punish her, but I need her to control her behavior if I am to successfully conduct class. Will you please speak with her and give me any suggestions for dealing with her in the future?" The positive effects of being proactive, as described here could lead to an ally in the parents and decrease the chances of a negative meeting in the future.

The second reaction could be much different. Cindy walked in the front door of the house and went directly to her room. Later, her parents sensed a problem and asked her what was bothering her. Cindy proceeded to tell her parents that she was disciplined for her behavior in class today. Further, the teacher said nothing to the other students who were misbehaving, and then the teacher threatened to send her to the office if she ever did it again!

As you can clearly see, the parents' information is quite different. Often, getting to the parents *first* can be the difference between a positive and negative interaction. It is amazing the number of individuals who will not make the initial call because it "could" be confrontational, when *not* calling almost always ensures a future meeting *will* be confrontational. The best advice: Be brave, be proactive, and make the call.

2. BE PREPARED AND BE ON TIME

It sounds so simple, yet this is arguably one of the main reasons for an *unsuccessful* meeting. I have had numerous meetings with staff who came to a parent meeting to discuss student performance in the classroom and provided no grades, data, or examples of student work to provide input. As an administrator, you must ensure staff members do not stroll in late or forget the meeting is taking place at all. It is not a good use of time for any participant involved to wait while a school personnel member is paged to attend the meeting. If you were to put yourself in the place of the parent, who may have had to take time from their work for the meeting, it would be easy to sense their frustration. This is especially compounded when the school or teacher may have initiated the meeting!

If the parent is present for academic reasons, be ready to have staff members explain their position and provide a foundation beyond mere professional judgment. It is amazing how many educators are offended that a parent would *dare* second-guess their judgment after possibly years of experience. In reality, we live in a nation that strongly encourages a "second opinion" whenever a physician diagnoses a problem; why would we as educators expect any different treatment? Further, most doctors provide x-rays, blood work, or test results when they make a diagnosis and still a second opinion may be sought. Of course, the parent will be skeptical when the teacher merely states, "He just doesn't seem to grasp the material" or "She seems to be somewhere else daydreaming when we cover the material in class."

To further illustrate this point, suppose the student's problem is in the English/language arts subject area. One suggestion would be to provide an example of the student's work to show the parents the problem with their son/daughter's writing. Further, provide them with two or three examples of good writing from other students in the class (without names listed, of course) with varied ability levels to illustrate the desired outcome for the grading or rubric. Do not make the mistake of comparing the top student's work to the student in question, as it is unfair to compare all students to the best. Utilize the work from an average student and make this fact evident to the parents. If the teacher or staff member does include the work from the top student in the class, work from lower performing students should be utilized as well. It is much easier for the parents to understand deficiencies if they are aware of the range in the classroom from the top to the bottom and are made aware of how their son/daughter falls in the grouping of the class.

The idea for providing student work and a comparison for desired outcomes can be utilized for every subject area in every grade level. It is not enough to merely state, "Johnny is not performing up to grade level and something needs to be done." It is much better and well-received when the school can stipulate, "Johnny is not performing up to the level of his peers. Here is an example of his work, and here are three examples of other students' work in the class. We need to take steps to ensure that he will catch up and be able to perform these outcomes as well as his classmates." It is much more difficult to argue when the data are present and the parents can visibly *see* what is expected.

When utilizing data for parent meetings, it is also important to be aware of other types of data used. For example, many districts utilize standardized tests in determining academic placement. These types of assessment may be utilized for special education services, talented and gifted services, or intervention classes for state mandates. It is *strongly* recommended that district overreliance on these tests does not develop.

Unfortunately, school personnel can become entrenched in the numbers game. For instance, when parents or guardians hear, "Your son/daughter scored in the bottom 10 percent of all U.S. students on the California Achievement Test," they have no idea what this entails. They may be wondering and afraid to ask what this represents and what material was tested. Initially, many questions will go through a parent's mind such as: "Is he slow?" "Is she behind?" "Does this mean she can't go to college?" "Will this mean he has to be retained?"

Parents may not ask questions initially due to embarrassment, lack of knowledge, or lack of time to process what they have just been told. Professionals must anticipate this and be ready to explain the answers to the questions *before* they are asked. It is much like teaching students in a classroom; experienced educators are well aware of the questions students will ask *before* they cover the material. The same experience should allow us to anticipate questions and put parents at ease when providing test results.

The previous example strategies were discussed for an academic meeting. What if the parents were called to discuss a discipline situation? As an assistant principal, there will be numerous opportunities for a negative meeting regarding a discipline issue.

Many times, a parent is "on guard" and feels this is an example of discrimination. It is easy for this type of meeting to become a finger-pointing meeting, and positive outcomes are impossible. The same strategies from academic meetings can be utilized under these conditions as well. For instance, in the primary grade levels, it may be possible to have a colleague collect data before the meeting begins. For example, suppose the student simply *cannot sit still* for any period of time. In today's fast-paced world, this is a typical problem for many students. It is best to have another school official sit in the child's classroom quietly in the back, charting the number of times "Johnny" is out of his seat or off-task. Do this for fifteen minutes and then conduct the same activity for two or three other students in the classroom (again, not the best students).

As before, when the data are placed in front of the parent, it is harder to argue and the unbiased third party alleviates the finger-pointing aspect of the meeting. Remember, it is best to educate, not alienate, the parents. Proper preparation is essential to achieving desired results. With time, most parents will reach the same conclusion as the school district; with data, you may be able to lead the parents to this end.

Further, allowing the parents to understand the school does not expect *perfection* may put the parents at ease. As school officials, we realize all students learn at a different pace, and academic meetings are usually required when students are performing well below the average range. Parents want to believe the school is reasonable in its expectations. Many times, it is a matter of *educating the parent* so the parent can learn where the child is deficient.

Too often, many administrators want to state the problem and immediately jump to a preordained plan. It is a big mistake to steamroll the parent and indicate, "This is what we are doing because we are the professionals and we know best." Parents do not wish to feel as though important decisions are made before they have entered the building. School officials may have an idea in mind, but flexibility is the key.

The importance of preparation and promptness for any meeting cannot be stressed enough. Knowing most parents are not argumentative does not suggest to only prepare for the meetings that could involve "potential problems." Professional educators have the responsibility to prepare for all meetings equally and "getting in the habit" of preparing thoroughly is a useful skill for the ease of all. Consider, practice, and role-play with the following case study to further illustrate the ideas discussed in strategy 2.

Case Study

Stacy has difficulties with her writing skills. She frequently misspells words and seldom uses proper punctuation or capitalization. Her teacher believes she has more ability than she has put forth, as the work appears "sloppy" and "hurried." Stacy realizes she has difficulties and is apprehensive about the subject matter. Further, she takes the poor marks personally and feels as though her poor grades are due to the fact that the teacher "dislikes her." Her parents are aware she struggles with language arts class as well, but feel as though the teacher grades their daughter too critically. A meeting has been scheduled to discuss Stacy's progress. In preparation for this meeting, consider the following questions:

1. What data could Stacy's teacher utilize to explain his/her position?
2. What strategies could have been utilized to assist Stacy with her difficulties?
3. For a moment, assume the role of the "hostile" parent. What statements would you expect to hear as you discuss the situation?
4. How do you think the school should address Stacy's poor academic standing?
5. What are some possible positive outcomes for the meeting? (Be certain to include the role of each participant in the meeting—the teacher, Stacy, and her parents.)

3. BE POLITE WITH AN INVITING SETTING

It may be difficult to believe, but many parents are either terrified or detest the idea of coming into the school, especially when they have been called in for a "meeting with the administration." When they enter the building, many parents complain of feeling as though they are "on trial" and make the statement, "They speak down to me as though I am a child." There are four aspects of the parent meeting that may make the parents feel more comfortable and may assist in conducting a productive meeting.

First, consider the *need* for the meeting in relation to *setting* and *location*, as the tone of a meeting is often set during the first moments in the room. It may not be appropriate to have a meeting to discuss the child's academic standing in the principal's office with the administrator sitting behind the desk in a "power" position.

If the meeting is regarding educational placement, academics, or interventions needed, a table in the counselor's office may assist in putting all the participants at ease. In this manner, the parents feel as though they are participants, not subordinates in the process. This may sound trivial, but negative perceptions are more likely to be encountered when individuals are uncomfortable.

This discussion does not suggest the school should *never* assume a "power position." For instance, if a student brought a knife to school and safety was an issue, the guidance counselor's table is probably not the best idea. In this situation, the parents need to understand the school will look out for the safety and well-being of all students, and parent comfort level is not a priority at that time. Remember, the need for the meeting should be weighed against the location and setting.

Second, consider the number of individuals involved in the meeting. It can be alarming for parents to enter a room to discuss their child and face five or six people with a variety of degrees and titles. The district should be aware of "educator overload," inviting extraneous personnel to the meeting for moral support of the facilitator. Unless it is a training process (which should be stated at the beginning of the meeting), there should never be more participants in the meeting than necessary for its success. Often, school personnel are alarmed when parents bring advocates (even clergy) into the room for support and wonder why those individuals are present. All participants—parents and educators—can potentially share these thoughts; if so, the participants are more likely to feel intimidated and less likely to contribute.

Consider the following example: A student was misbehaving repeatedly in class. "Ashley" happened to be a special education student and was placed in the regular classroom for the majority of the school day with one hour of instruction in a resource room. Ashley's parents were called for a meeting. When they entered the room they were greeted, politely, by the following individuals: her teacher, the special education teacher, the educational aide in the room (she witnessed the behavior), an intervention specialist (called for input and suggestions to eliminate the behavior), the assistant principal (as it was a discipline matter), and the guidance counselor serving as the facilitator. There were six school personnel present for a behavioral meeting that could have possibly been handled by the teacher. It is easy to see how the parents in this situation may initially be uncomfortable and become defensive, especially if the misbehavior was not severe in nature.

There may be an occasion for numerous individuals with input required, but the district should be aware that not every meeting requires a full-scale alert mentality. Further, this scenario illustrates the enormous amount of resources spent on this one, possibly minor, incident. These individuals could be assisting other staff and students, providing much needed support elsewhere.

The third aspect of this particular strategy is making the actual meeting space comfortable and "human." Think about how anxiety is heightened upon entering a sterile waiting room or examination room at the doctor's office. We as educators need to avoid this "lab coat syndrome." One meeting space suggestion is to include a small coffee pot with mugs, tea bags, and instant coffees, and parents are offered these prior to the meeting. A dish of candy, pads of paper, and pens could be on the table or close at hand for *all* participants' use. This contributes to a more relaxed feel without compromising any of the professionalism of the task at hand.

A final strategy to keep in mind is the need to be polite and professional. Start off by welcoming the parents and thanking them for attending. For the majority of parents, concessions were made to attend, and acknowledging the accommodations is important and proper etiquette. Some parents may make comments such as, "Well, I'm really not sure why I am here anyway—nothing I say is going to matter!" Administrators should anticipate this response and have an answer ready. An appropriate response would be, "That is simply untrue; we value your opinion or we would not have called—your assistance is very important in this process." The district is better served by reaching the desired results collegially with all participants feeling as though the well-being of the child and the school have been served.

Similarly, throughout the meeting the school staff should avoid what could be termed as "ed-speak." We as educators know there is an acronym for virtually every scenario we face. Imagine if you utilize terms such as IAT, IEP, IDEA, SBH, TBI, ED, and so on, and the parents in your meeting have no idea what these terms mean. Most people become reclusive when faced with the possibility of looking foolish. As a result, many parents fail to provide input when faced with educational vocabulary and acronyms that we as educators utilize daily.

Further, many parents may leave such a meeting feeling the district is uncaring and pretentious. You must always be leery of a meeting in which parents have provided little (if any) feedback. While this meeting may be efficient and expedient, the opportunity for negative feelings may be present. One suggestion is to simply state, "I apologize if you feel as though I am over-simplifying things, but I want to make certain you fully understand what we are discussing. Many times some parents do not understand, so I am going to put in simple terms all aspects of this situation." Without talking down to the parents, you must often educate all members of the family to be successful.

Consider the following scenario and discuss the questions provided with a mentor or administrative colleague.

Discussion Scenario

A teacher felt as though a student should be retained due to his poor effort and failing academic scores. You had met with his parents on numerous occasions and knew they would not agree with this decision. The principal asked you to lead a meeting with the child's teachers and parents regarding this situation.

- What do you feel the proper decision should be in this matter?
- Does your district have a policy regarding retention of students?
- Does the grade level of the student have any bearing in this scenario?
- How does the amount of previous parent-teacher communication affect your feelings in your decision?

4. FOLLOW A SUCCESSFUL MEETING PROTOCOL

The last suggestion to ensure a successful meeting is to follow a simple formula designed to make the meeting constructive, focused, and productive. These few simple steps will ensure the agenda for the conference is completed and progress is made.

First, know what you would like to accomplish when the meeting is scheduled. Too often parents are called to the school simply to be informed of problems, but no anticipated solution is expected. Alone, an informational meeting is seldom productive. Know what you would like to see happen, the bottom line. The purpose of the meeting must be known prior to the meeting, even if the means by which that purpose is accomplished shall be determined during the meeting itself.

Second, keep the meeting focused. As described previously, parents (and educators) have a tendency to lose focus and stray from the original intention of the meeting. Guard against this. Utilize the ideas discussed previously and progress toward the bottom line.

Third, develop an action plan to accomplish the goals for the meeting. When steps have been determined for success, it is important that a facilitator helps to determine the responsibilities for each person involved—parents, student, and faculty alike. If goals are to be accomplished, all parties involved must take an active role in the solution. If the meeting was in response to a discipline situation, amicably arrive at the decision and any behavioral plans that are appropriate. In any case, make certain all participants understand the tasks they are assigned and the methods of completing those tasks.

Lastly, set up any follow-up meetings necessary to ensure success. Often, a single meeting is appropriate for the initial planning, but other meetings may be necessary to measure progress and explore other methods of intervention. When setting up a future meeting, it is a courtesy to try to arrange it with the parent's schedule in mind. As educators, we sometimes seem to be quite rigid with time slots when we can meet with parents. Of course, our schedules, at times, are not flexible. But too often, staff members will make the comment, "The meeting will be at 7:30 a.m. before school starts or not at all. If the parents cannot attend, we will conduct the meeting without them." Some compromises are vital and must be reached. After all, most educators would expect the same from *their* children's teachers.

If the administrator adheres to the previous strategies, there is still no guarantee that each and every meeting scheduled will un-equivocally be positive and great results will always follow. Those types of claims would be unfounded and unrealistic. After all these steps have been taken, will there still be moments for frustrated parents to view the school negatively? Absolutely! This is under-stood and it is recommended that school administrators stick by their guns in matters that are best for the district *and* the student. There may be moments when parents are a hindrance to their own child's education. If the school personnel have followed these strategies and behaved in an ethical, impartial, professional man-ner while the parents still refuse to cooperate, the district is then obligated to perform its duties as an educational institution with the student's best interest in mind.

Utilizing the strategies discussed could assist in providing cohe-sion and structure, while eliminating many of the excuses parents have for being negative. Too often, we as educators are players in the excuse-eliminating business, and these strategies, if used earnestly, will assist in this process. Also, every parent who leaves the building feeling comfortable, appreciated, and heard will serve as a public relations asset for the district. Further, and more im-portant, positive parents increase the opportunity for student suc-cess. A student who perpetually hears at home why the school is in-effective or non-caring will seldom perform well academically and will cease to become an active participant in his/her education. Knowing the strong student implications, it is impossible to ignore the tremendous opportunities that strong parent communication can provide. A good suggestion would be for the entry-year ad-ministrator to follow this advice "Be the type of leader you would want for your own child."

II

STRATEGIES FOR MEETING WITH A NEGATIVE PARENT

Regardless of your preparation for a parent meeting, there is always an opportunity for hostility or negative feelings to develop. The assistant principal position, by its very nature, is sometimes set up to handle the negative parent. However, with some simple strategies and preparation, even the most negative parent can leave feeling "heard" and "respected" in the educational process. Experience has taught me that if you truly listen and respect the parents' opinion, the chances are greater both the needs of the student and the district can be met with an amicable solution. Discuss the following strategies with your mentor as you complete the remainder of this chapter.

1. SEPARATE THE ACTION FROM THE STUDENT

Often, heated parent meetings are the result of some discipline issue. If there is a day-to-day problem in the classroom, the strategies discussed in the previous chapter may prove most helpful. If the parents are called for an *isolated* incident, it is important to make the parents understand the issue to be addressed does not imply they have failed as parents or their child is now destined for failure. While this may seem overly dramatic, many parents take the actions of their children personally and sometimes a little reassurance makes all the difference.

When dealing with the student, it is often helpful to remind them we must deal with what the student did and move on. Parents and students must understand actions are choices and these choices lead to consequences, but being young is about making mistakes, and education is about teaching students lessons both *in* and *out* of the classroom. As an entry-year administrator, there were often moments when I had occasion to inform students, "Unfortunately, today you forced me to do the worst part of my job—discipline." Further, "Just because I may not *like* to deal with discipline issues does not imply that I will not."

After a situation has been addressed, it is proper to make the parents realize that what the student did is not a reflection of who they are or who they will be. Education extends beyond the classroom; parents must understand this includes discipline issues. Successful school districts seek to *change behavior* when addressing discipline issues rather than merely *punish* participants.

Often, negative discipline meetings occur when the district is punishing students for behavior the parents feel is justified. It is common for parents to make the statement, "He did exactly what I have instructed him to do in that situation!" The experienced administrator or school official has a response to this statement. For instance they could state, "I appreciate that, but because he reacted that way I am forced to follow school policy and address the situation. If you are going to insist he behave in this manner, at the very least, prepare him to deal with the consequences of that behavior."

Further, in discipline situations, often the meeting is ended with the administering of the punishment. Ending the meeting in this manner can lead to hard feelings and these feelings can fester and lead to a future heated meeting. It is helpful to end a meeting with a "Where do we go from here?" approach. After the student has been disciplined, the student and the parents need to understand the child will not be blackballed upon returning to the building or classroom. Reassure all parties the issue is settled and has been addressed.

Most important, provide the student strategies to deal with inquisitive peers in the days ahead. School personnel must understand the child will be bombarded with questions such as, "What happened?" or "What did they do to you?" Experience tells us these questions will come. If we truly care about the welfare of the student and the culture of the school, we must arm the students with the means to address these issues. In taking the extra step, parents will observe that you care enough to help alleviate these moments, and they will see that the district is trying to *educate, not punish,* their child. If parents truly believe that education is the district goal, it will leave a lasting positive impression that will pay large dividends in relieving negative, hostile feelings.

2. AVOID SIBLING COMPARISONS

When an administrator has been in a district long enough, it is quite common to work with several children from the same family. Often, those children behave quite differently in the educational setting. Parents know this as well. If a student's older brother or sister was exceptional, that student may feel inferior and detest the thought of the comparisons. Conversely, if the older sibling was a nightmare for the school, the parents and the student may be guarded against false first impressions and act defensively when hearing from the school district.

Avoid statements like, "I was so surprised to see this out of her. Her sister would have never behaved this way," or "I was expecting him to get much better grades after seeing what his brother could accomplish." Statements like this can potentially inflame an already defensive parent and bring about an undesired reaction. Further, as educators we understand the differences that are evident in children, even within the same family.

It is also important to make parents aware of the danger of making these comparisons themselves. If you hear a parent expressing frustration, assure them sibling differences are normal and one child's behavior can never be a predictor for another.

This strategy is not meant to imply that school personnel should shy away from making conversation; reliving successful stories with older siblings can ease the tension in a stressful meeting. Further, asking about the progress or status of older siblings shows care and concern on the part of the school district and subconsciously reminds parents the situation is not personal because the other sibling had a successful tenure with the district. Rather, this strategy is included as an item to be aware of when a negative parent may be entering the office, especially if the older sibling was difficult and required much intervention for success.

3. UTILIZE THE PARENT(S) AS A RESOURCE

Parents may be the most underutilized resource for most school districts. One reason for this is the assumption that the parents and educators will enter the meeting with differing opinions. In the case of the negative parent, the perception is that the district may be erroneous in any judgment of their son/daughter. The district often has the perception that the parents are "spoiling" the child and supporting them at all costs. The simple truth is both may, in fact, be partially correct.

Both parties must realize, just as school employees act differently outside the school setting, children are totally different when they have peers to impress or compete against for the teacher's attention. Parents are sometimes shocked when they receive reports of misbehavior and actions they never have witnessed. While in the home, most children have their parents' attention. The ratio of child to adult in most homes is often two to one or even less in some situations. Children, while in the home setting, potentially are under a more watchful eye and may not have as much freedom to behave in negative ways.

Parents must be made to understand their children will behave much differently when peers are present. The need for peer approval is very strong in the school setting. School personnel are wise to explain this and do so in a non-condescending manner. The purpose of most negative meetings is to change something in the child's placement or address some negative behavior. These can be alarming scenarios for most parents. The school must reinforce repeatedly that any changes are not made to make life easier for the school district; changes are made for future success and opportunities for the child.

If the district considers the parents as the "experts" at home and parents would recognize the district serves as the "expert" while in the school setting, the meetings are more likely to be successful. During most intervention meetings with school personnel, ideas are exchanged for the best manner in teaching a student. Quality teachers, counselors, and administrators routinely brainstorm ideas for the success of students. No one teacher should be expected to have all the answers. Educational dialogue is paramount for professional growth! Leaving the one-room school house centuries ago allowed for collegial discussion, which still is inadequately utilized in many instances.

In this collaboration, consider the perception of the parents. They are entering into the school and expecting some professional to "tell them about their child." The parents feel as though they already know their child, and they have years of experience in dealing with him/her. Further, their experience started first! Realizing this may make it easier to understand the defensive nature of many parents. When district personnel begin to understand this parent perspective, they may be better prepared to address the negative parent in a school meeting. Incidentally, parents may provide insight of which school personnel was previously unaware. If this is the case, be certain to thank the parents for the input and the information.

If the school district were to ask the parents during the course of the meeting, "You see them every evening; do you see this behavior at home?" or "You know him better than anyone; how does he learn best?" These types of questions call on the *expertise* of the parents and immediately give them some respect. Human nature allows for the guard to come down when respect has been issued. Further, the district may receive some suggestions that could be beneficial in educating the child.

This strategy is not meant to suggest that school personnel allow the parents to determine placement or the consequences of misbehavior, but ignoring the opportunity for assistance is shortsighted on the part of the district.

4. FIND SOMETHING POSITIVE

In this era where political correctness has become a negative concept, this strategy may not be popular. Often administrators desire to tell it like it is. Unfortunately, as most school districts rely on voter support, this potential alienation may ultimately hinder other educational programs. Focusing on some positive aspect could have a long lasting impact, though it may at times involve a creative approach.

For instance, if a child is the "leader of the pack" and the pack is behaving improperly, parents need to be informed. There are several ways to address the issue with the parents. For instance, school personnel could say, "Mr. and Mrs. Jones, thank you for attending today's meeting. It appears as though your son is behaving improperly and even getting others to go along with him. We cannot have this and he is bringing others down with his bad example."

Another approach could be, "Mr. and Mrs. Jones, first of all, thanks for coming in today. We would like to discuss some things we are observing with your son. He is a natural leader. Other students seem to take right to him and follow his example. This is positive for him, and we would like your help in getting him to be a positive role model for his peers. At this point, they do as he does and once in a while, we have some behavior incidents."

While the examples cited are simplistic, they do illustrate an important point. Children and parents alike need some form of positive reinforcement. If the district utilizes the first technique, the parents may feel as though the school believes they are responsible for their child's behavior, or they may feel attacked by the district. Remember, as discussed previously, they may not see these behaviors at home, as children act differently in different settings.

Many educators may claim, "Why should we find something positive when the child is acting negatively? Why reward the bad behavior?" This argument may have some merit *if* one fails to understand exactly how this strategy is to be utilized. There should be no implication that the district should reinforce bad behavior. Quite the contrary, the district is applauded for having the meeting to correct the behavior. It is simply worth noting that parents are more likely to become allies if they feel as though the school district or its personnel are not discriminating against their child.

In the situation above, citing leadership ability as a positive trait is appropriate. Obviously, if other students are following his/her lead, he is a natural leader. Further, in our society, leadership skills are widely appreciated. And finally, many behavioral specialists would reinforce the need to channel students to the desired behavior as opposed to simply punishing the undesirable behavior. Remember, the ultimate goal is to educate the child, and alienating the parents cannot assist in this process.

Suppose for a moment the meeting was regarding the retention of a student rather than a discipline issue. What can be positive about prohibiting a student from moving forward with his peers? Again, the *issue* may not be positive, but there are undoubtedly items the child has performed well throughout the year. If the child is well behaved and attentive in class, this must be brought to the meeting at some point.

Positive comments bring parents on your side, and when all parties have the same focus (in this situation, the child's education), good decisions will be made. Never fail to remember the value of positive comments: "I really like your son or daughter, but I just do not feel as though he/she is ready to progress to the next grade level and here are the data to support my belief." The initial phrasing cannot be understated; "I like him/her" will make the parents feel as though the issue is not personal.

Sincerity is important, though—educators should not make glowing statements if they do not believe what they are saying. Past actions will likely contradict these statements and reduce the believability of the suggestions at the meeting. Overall, if the teacher or school personnel does truly *like* the student, stating this can add to the meeting. Conversely, if the staff member does *not* seem to connect with the student, it is probably best to not mention this fact during the course of the meeting. Any educator, especially those who are also parents, can appreciate the value of receiving positive comments regarding their child.

5. BE PROFESSIONAL AT ALL COSTS

Negative parents may say things during the course of the meeting they later regret. Entry-year administrators should be cautioned against doing the same. Staying in control, not losing your temper, and staying focused on the purpose of the meeting all sound like common sense, but they are easier said than done in many situations. School personnel may become frustrated at the concept of having to listen to a parent or guardian vent while being required to maintain composure. While these frustrations exist, it is still in our professional mandates as educators. It is important to keep in mind, for the parents the issue may be personal. This is their child, their family, or their reputation. For the educator, the issue is in the realm of our profession—our work. While we sometimes take our work personally (and good administrators often do), we must guard against reacting with personal attacks or vindictiveness.

This by no means implies that educators should sit and be the victims of personal attacks. There is a distinct difference between a frustrated comment and a tirade or intimidating gestures. If the latter is the case, the administrator is strongly urged to professionally end the meeting by stating, "If you are going to speak to me in this manner, this meeting is over! You may leave or we will be forced to contact the authorities!" No one should be the victim of verbal abuse, but being professional in the face of negative parents is not the same as abuse; it is vital the distinction is made.

The off-the-cuff comments, possibly regarding other students in the class or the teacher, should always be handled calmly. You should, in the face of these comments, ask for specifics. If they are accusations and they are unfounded, return the focus of the meeting to the task at hand. I suggest a statement such as, "We will address your concerns, and I may need to talk with you more in depth regarding this issue, but for now we really need to focus on the reason you are here and that is . . . " If the accusations or comments are serious in nature and appear to have merit, then the administration needs to be involved, and a private meeting should be arranged at a later time with the parents and necessary personnel.

6. DON'T GET CAUGHT UP IN THEIR NEGATIVITY

In many ways, this discussion is an extension of the last strategy. It is amazing the number of occasions where a parent is negative or upset with the school and their anger has nothing to do with the meeting that brought them to school. For instance, the parents may be unhappy with the coach who did not play their child enough in the athletic contests and this anger spills over to the teacher or the administrator conducting the meeting. There are moments when your meeting is an opportunity to reestablish faith in the school setting in the face of some other dilemma.

Often, parents will attempt to inadvertently change the focus of the meeting. In the example just given, the school personnel may call the parents regarding an academic issue, and the parents will attempt to take the conversation down another path. Parents will sometimes make the comment, "Well, I wanted him to keep his grades up as well. We worked really hard to be eligible for basketball, and with the way the season is going, he is too frustrated to keep trying. Do you know what that coach is doing?" This is a common occurrence for many administrators when meeting with parents, and while you may be sympathetic, you should really do your best to ensure the meeting stays on track.

It is important for the administrator to give the parent the brief moment to vent, but then steer them away from this. You might try this approach: "That is unfortunate. Did you speak with the coach or athletic director about your concerns?" Most of the time the parents have not or will not take this advice. Still, some will make the comment, "It will not do any good anyway." At this point you could say, "You might be surprised. If you feel that strongly, you should do so. *Now let's get back to the purpose of the meeting.*"

In the scenario described above, the assistant principal listened and appeared concerned. Frequently, this is the main objective of the negative parent. They would like someone to listen to their point of view. Again, providing this service, if kept in check, is good for the district and the overall purpose of your meeting. As stated previously, however, there is a fine line between listening and losing the focus of the meeting. There is also a fine line between keeping the meeting on track and appearing unsympathetic. The point is that you try to do both—listen but keep the meeting moving.

Another strategy that works well in this arena is asking a question related to your cause. For instance, if the parent refuses to stick to the topic of the discussion and continually focuses on past issues, consider asking a question that requires them to *think* about your topic. If the parents perpetually say, "Well, if you had not done this. . . " or "If the teacher had not done that . . . " the experienced administrator could respond, "I understand your concerns. Do you think Johnny is not doing well because of lack of effort or lack of understanding?" You then might ask, "How much time does he spend on his studies each evening?" The parents now must think and answer your questions—this enables you to keep the focus on *your* topic of conversation.

Overall, it is important for the entry-year administrator to remember *you* called the meeting; therefore, *you* are in control of the meeting. If positive outcomes are to happen, they will only do so under the proper structure.

PRACTICE YOUR ANTICIPATION SKILLS

Often the art of conducting a positive meeting in a negative environment involves the ability to anticipate the negative reaction from a seemingly trivial circumstance. If you are able to predict negative feedback, many times school personnel will be better equipped to address concerns of the parents. Consider the following scenarios and be prepared to cite possible conclusions. Although there are no right answers, an entry-year administrator should work to develop the skills necessary to anticipate the frustrated and negative parent. Review the following scenarios with your mentor and determine the actions necessary to conduct a positive parent meeting.

Scenario 1

Susie raised her hand and asked the teacher to go to the restroom. The teacher stated, "Not right now, you may go in a few minutes." Susie's parents called the school the next day and demanded a meeting with the teacher and the administration.

- Why would her parents be so upset with the teacher?
- Are there examples the teacher could provide to justify the delay of restroom privileges?

Scenario 2

Johnny told his parents he would receive bonus points in his class if he took extra paper in for classroom activities. His parents called the school to complain. Why?

- What is the probable reason for their complaint?
- Can the teacher explain the situation in an acceptable manner?

Scenario 3

After three previous warnings due to excessive noise in the classroom, the teacher told her class, "The next person to cause a class disruption will receive a discipline referral." Tim, who is usually a good student and well behaved, was leaning over to assist a fellow classmate with the assignment. The teacher saw him talking and immediately reprimanded him. The next day his parents requested a meeting with the teacher and his counselor.

- What do you think they wish to discuss?
- Utilizing the strategies discussed previously, prepare for the meeting.

Scenario 4

Amy was reading well below grade level and her peers. The teacher felt as though she needed extensive intervention and possible retention. She was the lowest performing student in the classroom.

- Utilizing the strategies in the manual, outline a meeting with her parents—be certain to include location, personnel, and a possible action plan.

Scenario 5

Kyle was an above-average middle school student and worked very diligently in his coursework. He was involved in some extracurricular activities, but not as many as some of his peers. Recently, he was *not* inducted into his school's chapter of the National Junior Honor Society. His parents demanded a meeting with the advisor and the school counselor or administration.

- Using the previous strategies, formulate a discussion with his parents.
- Is it possible to have a positive meeting in this manner, or should the parents just "accept things the way they are?" Explain.

Scenario 6

Derrick was a hard worker, but he did not make the school's basketball team. His parents had taken the position that he was talented but "the coach had it out for him" and didn't want him on the team.

- Can the strategies be utilized in a sports setting? If so, how?
- Which of the strategies discussed previously apply most to this meeting?

Scenario 7

Jamie was extremely bright and her teacher was attempting to challenge her due to her well-above-average abilities. The teacher was attempting to ask more of Jamie than some of her peers. Consider Jamie's perspective in this matter and the thoughts her parents may have as a result.

- How should the teacher explain her position should a meeting take place?
- What preparation could make this scenario easier to explain and/or prevent a negative meeting from ever taking place?

⑫

WORKING WITH TEACHERS AND CLASSROOM MANAGEMENT

Discipline and classroom management have roots in ISLLC standards 2, 3, 4, and 5. School personnel must always keep perspective in addressing the misbehavior of students. For instance, all decisions require the professional administrator to be fair and impartial when addressing students who have disrupted the learning process. Although the above standards were designed for administrators, they are no less important to the classroom teacher in day-to-day situations.

Nevertheless, it can be difficult to address discipline issues and classroom management with various staff members. Teachers desire varying levels of autonomy. Some ask often for a helping hand in the classroom while others may never ask. The reason for the differences could be many, including the subject area taught, years of teaching experience, and levels of tolerance. Because educators are human, these differences are natural. However, these differences can also send inconsistent messages to the students and create dissonance.

The assistant principal will soon discover one of the major complaints by students and community is the widely held belief that certain individuals, based on any one of several criteria, receive *special* treatment. For instance, do the students at your school believe the sons/daughters of school board members receive the same treatment as everyone else? Do they (the students) perceive students of a different race get treated the same? What about other criteria such as socioeconomic status, athletic ability, appearance, or intelligence? Prepared teachers and administrators are instrumental in alleviating this special treatment belief.

All school personnel can attest to the fine line between treating all students *fairly* and treating all students *equally*. This can be difficult, and at times, stressful. Every decision made has the potential for scrutiny, and the administrator's integrity and judgment could be called into question. To make the situation more difficult, the administrative action may need to be taken with no advance notice and no amount of preparation.

To combat some of these situations, all administrators are strongly encouraged to work with staff and develop a preventative approach to discipline issues. Knowing that every teacher is unique and every classroom can be managed differently are key components of the informed and knowledgeable instructional leader. There is no substitute for quality staff members who make well-informed decisions and practice good judgment.

To begin, since new teachers have the most difficulty transitioning to the new position, a recommendation is to meet periodically with those new faculty members and address questions/issues they may have. Most bad habits exhibited by veteran teachers are established over many years; thus, it is best to begin molding and nurturing good and desirable habits in new teachers to the profession. After you have worked with new faculty to the building—over time—you will have a staff that fully understands your expectations, and you will have fewer issues to address with faculty. Some examples of topics to cover may include:

- inclusion and the best practices to utilize with special education students
- final/semester exams (if appropriate at your grade level)
- mentor program (if this is a process for first-year employees in your district)
- lesson planning—formation/documentation
- discipline issues—provide examples and have *quality* discussion of your expectations
- assessment—this includes standardized and individual classroom
- questioning techniques in the classroom
- evaluation procedures
- professional dress and attire
- include other topics as you see items that need addressed

New faculty will undoubtedly benefit from this coaching in learning the procedures and policies of the building. While veteran teachers may desire and actually *deserve* more autonomy in their classrooms, new teachers should have more guidance and direction in the early years of their career. They will likely face more issues and have more questions during the course of the school year. As an entry-year administrator, you may not feel knowledgeable to address all of these questions as they arise. A quality meeting and discussion format can be a great learning experience for the administrator and the teacher. Both can gather pertinent information, learn on the job, and develop a rapport for which a solid foundation can be built for future issues.

The next step in developing a preventative approach with personnel is realizing veteran staff members also need to be aware of how classroom management issues affect the administrative role and the building climate. If you were to travel from one classroom to the next in your building, you may see a variety of expectations regarding the disciplinary process. Usually, the larger issues are not as scrutinized, and all faculty and staff usually agree in how they would handle the situation.

Often the smaller issues that arise on a daily basis can create the most havoc on the learning process. For instance, most classrooms (hopefully) have a rule against large infractions such as fighting, profanity, and disrespect. These rules are typically uniform across the school, and students can expect to hear all teachers warn of punishment by not abiding by any of these, which are typically listed in all student handbooks. It is often the smallest of infractions that tend to catch students and create conflict in the classroom.

To illustrate this point, I would make the following suggestion. Create a focus group of seven to ten teachers to work through and address their methods of handling the following classroom management topics:

- classroom lateness
- incomplete homework
- sharpening of a pencil
- asking a question of the teacher
- make-up work and tests
- cheating on homework/tests
- talking to another student during a class discussion
- failure to bring supplies to class (books, paper, writing utensil, etc.)
- group work
- restroom breaks during class

This same discussion process can be repeated for many other facets of classroom instruction. For instance, using the same focus group previously utilized, discuss the following questions.

- How should special education accommodations on tests and quizzes be handled?

- Should extra credit work or assignments be accepted?
- Do you "help" the student who has a 64.4 percent and needs a 65 percent to pass—if they are (a) a good, well-mannered student or (b) a chronic misbehaving student?
- Do you curve grades when a large group of students does poorly?
- How often should group work be utilized in the classroom?
- How should group work be graded?
- Are certain assignments or grades weighted for more point values?
- Should homework be graded? If so, how heavily is it considered in the grading process?

Compare the answers from each topic, and you will soon discover all teachers may handle these items differently. It takes some time for each student to discover what may be permissible in period two is not allowed in period three. The small discrepancies are the items that can cause the most confusion for students and the most stress for staff.

When you begin to analyze the differences between staff members, it is easy to see how students can become frustrated over the differing expectations and the methods in which classroom discipline can be administered. Also, the entry-year administrator must realize all of these discrepancies have the potential to become a parent meeting to discuss displeasure with the building/district. Thus, if the extra time is taken to prepare staff members and establish a clear understanding of the need for all to work collaboratively for the benefit of each student, more education can take place.

This training should be handled carefully. It is important, as you begin to work with classroom teachers, to understand there is no *one* technique to solving classroom management issues. In his 1994 book, *Preventing Classroom Discipline Problems, A Guide for Educators*, Howard Seeman points out that "it is insufficient to train teachers in *technique alone*" (p. 14).

If the entry-year administrator tries to instill rules or practices for addressing classroom discipline, he/she may soon discover many staff members have no difficulty with the changes while other staff members struggle mightily. This is due to the personality of the teachers and the degree to which their personality affects the techniques utilized. In fact, as Seeman states, the "technique is as effective as it is congruent to the teacher who employs it" (p. 15).

The more successful administrators will resist making statements such as, "When I taught, I did it this way and maybe you should try that approach." The role of administrator will provide you with the opportunity to watch countless teachers manage their classrooms. One of the most amazing aspects of this opportunity is studying and understanding the vast differences in which they operate while still accomplishing success in their individual classrooms. Remember as an assistant principal, you have moved into a role of "teacher of teachers" and just as no one classroom is filled with identical students, no one staff will be filled with identical teachers.

Realizing that it is acceptable to have individuals on staff with varying abilities and styles, the administrator must realize it is not acceptable if this individuality leads to student confusion. The role of the administrator is to require all staff to set clear and defined expectations for student behavior in their individual classrooms and to expect staff to follow board policies and procedures if appropriate. Treating all students fairly *does not* imply all teachers enforce uniform rules and procedures. Rather, treating all students fairly *does* require that all students understand the rules in the classroom, understand the consequences for violating those rules, and understand that all students will be held equally accountable.

Reflect on your time as a classroom teacher and answer the following questions:

- Did you have rules/policies that were unique for your classroom setting? If so, list those rules.

- Referring to the previous question, assume the role of the administrator in the building. Would you support the teacher if it were needed in the discipline of a student for one of those rules? Why or why not?

No discussion of classroom management is complete unless it involves addressing the teacher's effectiveness in the process. Good classroom management is a requirement if quality education is to take place. In examining this issue, the administrator must first make a key distinction. Is the teacher *capable* of effectively managing the classroom? If the teacher is capable and not performing to a satisfactory administrative level, discipline or motivation may be necessary. If the teacher is not capable of performing the tasks necessary for success, then termination may be necessary. In this case, a thorough understanding of the master agreement between the teachers' association and the board of education is required (if applicable).

Often, if veteran teachers are less than effective, they may be in a rut and merely need to be inspired or motivated. Bringing shortcomings to the teacher's attention *alone* may solve the problem. All of us need motivating at some point in our careers, and this can be accomplished, especially if those individuals who work around us are motivated in their work lives.

Chase and Chase (1993) provide excellent advice for new teachers, that also holds true for the new assistant principal: if you want to motivate, "be motivated yourself" (p. 27). Unless you cannot avoid the situation, do not ask the staff to complete tasks that you would not do yourself and encourage them to follow this example in their individual classrooms. When at all possible, try to be an asset to the teachers and assist by eliminating barriers that hinder progress. It can be amazing how the little things such as providing supplies or volunteering to help with a lesson can build rapport with staff and pay dividends later when other issues arise.

Another effective method of motivation is utilizing staff meetings and ceremonies to acknowledge outstanding staff service or effort. For example, some districts have award ceremonies or recognition dinners. Time and effort should be given to prepare for these occasions in order to stress their importance to your faculty. If your building does not have such traditions, work with your principal to create them! You should never miss an opportunity to reward and honor great teaching.

If a staff member is not capable of effectively managing his/her classroom, no amount of motivation will change the classroom climate to allow education to take place. All administrators should realize their first responsibility is to the students in the building! It is in this context that you are reminded to have the ability to effectively utilize the master contract for the benefit of the students in your district and building.

As an entry-year administrator, it is imperative that you express any staff issues with the principal if you believe termination is warranted. Ultimately, it is the principal who will make employment recommendations at the building level, but it is the assistant who will work closely with staff in issues involving students. As is true of most topics in this manual, discipline issues also illustrate the importance of good communication between all administrative personnel.

Consider the following scenarios and be prepared to answer the questions that follow.

1. A well-respected and veteran teacher brought a student into your office. She was in tears and made the comment, "That's it, I'm done!" You knew that her class was filled with twenty at-risk students and that one particular student was the ringleader and caused the most distractions. Many of the students were involved in the legal system, had parole officers, and had been in your office on numerous occasions.
   - Do you believe this is an issue of teacher capability or teacher support? Why or why not?

- How do you provide support for your staff member?
- How do you deal with the student who is misbehaving?
- What programs does your current district have to assist with these types of at-risk students?

2. Read the following scenario and complete the role-play that follows. A staff member entered your office and complained that the students in his class refused to follow the directions or adhere to classroom management rules. This particular staff member was repeatedly late to school, missed administrative deadlines, and conducted a classroom that lacked variety and differentiated instruction.

Role Play: Assume the role of the administrator and ask your mentor or colleague to assume the role of the teacher. List your suggestions for the teacher to garner control of the classroom? Would you address the shortcomings of the teacher? If so, how? Would your approach to the situation change based on the experience of the teacher? If so, how?

Assisting staff with classroom management is not an easy task. It can be cumbersome and confrontational on some occasions. If you are new to the building, it is imperative that you cultivate relationships before you make judgments on a teacher's ability (or lack of ability) to manage the classroom.

Overall, classroom management issues serve as a prime example of one of the most difficult aspects of administration—your day depends on the ability of the individuals you govern to do their jobs! Cultivating staff relationships effectively can greatly reduce your frustration level. It is important to remember this cultivation process must begin the first day of school in your first year of administration.

13

ADDITIONAL SCENARIOS AND DISCUSSION TOPICS

While the mentor and the entry-year administrator may not find the opportunity to read and discuss all the scenarios that follow, it is important for the regular meetings to provide professional growth opportunities for the entry-year administrator. Again, I do not mean to imply the situations described can replace real-life experiences, but they can assist in the preparation for the assistant by engaging in thought-provoking dialogue with an experienced administrator. It is important for the mentor and the assistant to view the scenarios as a starting point to examine existing policies for *their* district or position. Therefore, examining the following situations for a *correct* answer should not be the ultimate goal, as policies and practices vary from state to state and district to district. Rather, the goal should be for the mentor and the entry-year administrator to use the discussions to become more familiar with state regulations and district policies.

DISCUSSION SCENARIO I

A female student entered the office and asked for a private meeting. During this meeting, she disclosed the fact that she thought

she was pregnant and needed advice. She requested that you tell
no one of this discussion, as you are the first to know. She further
stated, "I am uncertain as to who the father is because I have been
with two boys in the past month."

- What advice should you give the student?
- Should you keep the discussion confidential per the student's
  request?
- What action should be taken by the assistant principal in this
  scenario?

DISCUSSION SCENARIO 2

The entry-year administrator in a neighboring district is frustrated
with her first administrative position. She believed she was never
given any projects that would enable her to become a principal and
run her own building in the future. She felt as though the principal was holding her back due to her entry-year status and lack of
experience. Further, there had been moments when the principal
asked for her opinion and taken credit for her ideas when they
later proved successful.

- Should she address this issue with her building level principal?
- Cite some suggestions you would give a colleague if he/she
  were in this situation.

DISCUSSION SCENARIO 3

A teacher in your building approached you and expressed concern for the well-being of one of her students. She believed the
student was being physically abused and was looking for your

guidance. She was able to cite specific examples and had some documentation for those examples. The teacher stated that she had gone to the counselor and he replied, "You must be mistaken, I know the family and there is no need to worry about them!"

- What advice do you give the teacher?
- Are there legal requirements for this scenario? If so, what are they?
- Should the principal be informed of this situation?
- Would this situation change if the student in question were the son/daughter of a school board member?
- How do you address the comments made by the guidance counselor?

DISCUSSION SCENARIO 4

An elderly man entered the office and asked for a moment of your time. He was a resident of the district and was concerned over what he saw as as waste of school tax dollars. He explained that he saw the lights of the school on every night in every classroom and had witnessed the windows open when the air conditioning is running. He further stated that he had supported the schools in their levy campaigns, but unless his concerns were addressed, he would no longer vote yes on school issues. He realizes that you are a new administrator and hopes that you will be more supportive than your predecessor, as his complaints always seemed to "fall on deaf ears."

- What do you say to the gentlemen regarding his concerns?
- Do you take any action regarding this issue?
- Would the situation change if this were a letter rather than a face-to-face visit? What if the complaints were anonymous?

DISCUSSION SCENARIO 5

You discover from a colleague that one of your staff members has been discussing your decision involving a school discipline issue. Apparently, this staff member had been complaining to other staff members that your decisions are too lenient and the students are more disrespectful to the teachers as a result.

- What do you do with the information you have been given?
- Should you trust stories you hear through the "grapevine?"
- Should you discuss this with the principal of the building?
- Does the ability of the teacher making the comments have any bearing on your dealings in this scenario?

DISCUSSION SCENARIO 6

Several staff members have made the comment, "You handle discipline so well and are so helpful for the teachers; you should be the principal!" You understand this feeling is starting to spread among some of the staff members.

- How do you deal with the comments made by the staff members?
- Should you address the comments with the principal?

DISCUSSION SCENARIO 7

The principal asked you to be the lead in a new teacher initiative. Teachers will be forced to change their presentation of lesson plans and a much greater amount of information will be required. These changes involve greater responsibilities and paperwork for the teaching staff and you know they will be very apprehensive regarding this process. Further, you do not feel as though this new system will improve student achievement and will only alienate you from the staff. You have met with the principal and he states, "I appreciate your input, but you will need to take the reins and complete the task I have assigned you."

- How should you handle this situation?
- What if staff members approach you and ask your opinion regarding this new approach to lesson planning?

DISCUSSION SCENARIO 8

A staff member entered your office at the end of the day. Apparently, as she was cleaning her room after the students were dismissed, she found a folded note on the floor. As she read the note, she became alarmed because it contained the following line, "Yes, I hate him too, we should kick his ass tomorrow." The teacher believed the note was passed between two students, but she cannot be certain, as she did not actually see the note being passed.

- What do you do with this information?
- If you believe you know which student was to be injured/threatened, what steps do you take for his protection?
- At what point in this scenario are the parents informed?
- What is your district policy regarding threatening or intimidating notes/gestures?
- Do you think recent school events have changed the manner in which schools address these types of incidents?

DISCUSSION SCENARIO 9

As the year was winding down and the summer was approaching, you received a phone call. It was the principal of another district and he was inquiring about one of your staff members.

The recommendation would be for a teacher who had little classroom control and who you believed to be one of the weaker staff members in your building. You understand that losing this staff member would be beneficial to your students and the staff, but are uncertain as to the proper way to answer the principal's questions.

- How would you answer a question regarding the teacher's employability skills?
- Is it ethical to provide only the *positive* attributes the teacher possesses?
- Are there legal considerations with this scenario?
- What if the teacher had previously informed you this call would be forthcoming and asked for your assistance in getting this position?

DISCUSSION SCENARIO 10

Just before school was to start, a parent entered your office and inquired about her daughter's teachers for the upcoming school year. You inform the parent who the student will have as a teacher and the parent is instantly agitated. The girl's mother then informed you she already had one child in that classroom and will not endure that teacher again.

- How do you address the mother's concerns?
- Is the fact that the parent already had one child in that teacher's class relevant?
- What are the repercussions for the building if you grant the mother's request? What are the repercussions for the district if you do not grant her request?

REFERENCES

AmeriCorps. (2006). *Parent-pals.com special education guide*. Retrieved November 2005, from http://parentpals.com/gossamer/pages/.

Chase, C. M., & Chase, J. E. (1993). *Tips from the trenches: America's best teachers describe effective classroom methods*. Lancaster, PA: Technomic.

Council of Chief State School Officers. (1996). *ISLLC Standards for school leaders*. Retrieved July 6, 2004, from http://www.ccsso.org.

Danielson, C. (1996). *Enhancing professional practice: A framework for teaching*. Alexandria, VA: Association for Supervision and Curriculum Development.

Donovsky, N. (2005). *Case law review*. Paper presented at the Ohio School Board Association Conference in Columbus, OH.

Lerner, J. (2000). *Learning disabilities: Theories, diagnosis, and teaching strategies* (8th ed.). Boston, MA: Houghton Mifflin.

Lindley, F. A. (2003). *The portable mentor: A resource guide for entry-year principals and mentors*. Thousand Oaks, CA: Corwin Press.

Ohio Department of Education. (2000). *Model policies and procedures for the education of children with disabilities*. Columbus, OH: Ohio Department of Education.

Rutherford Institute. (n.d.). *Teachers' rights in public education*. Retrieved August 16, 2006, from http://www.rutherford.org/pdf/teachers -rights.pdf.

Schoenfeld Crotty, E. (2006). *Legal update*. Paper presented at the Miami County Administrators Summer Conference, Piqua, OH.

Seeman, H. (1994). *Preventing classroom discipline problems: A guide for educators* (2nd ed.). Lancaster, PA: Technomic.

Tinker v. Des Moines Independent Community School District. (2006). *Wikipedia*. Retrieved August 14, 2006, from http://en.wikipedia.org/ wiki/Tinker_v._Des_Moines.

Villari, Brandes, & Kline, P. C. (n.d.). *IDEA: Special education lawyers protecting your child's rights*. Retrieved November 2005, from http://www .specialeducationlawyers.info/index.htm

ABOUT THE AUTHOR

Chad Mason began his career in 1994 after graduating with his B.S./B.A. from Ohio Northern University. He obtained his master's degree in educational administration in 1999 from the University of Dayton and then received his superintendent's licensure in 2000, also from the University of Dayton.

Mr. Mason has nearly fifteen years in education, with seven of those in the administrative ranks. During this time, he has served as a high school business teacher, a varsity girls' basketball coach, academic team advisor, high school assistant principal, and high school principal.

He is currently a member of the Ohio Association of Secondary School Administrators (OASSA) and the National Association of Secondary School Administrators (NASSP).

Mr. Mason is married and has one son. He and his family currently reside in Troy, Ohio, where he serves as principal of an area high school.